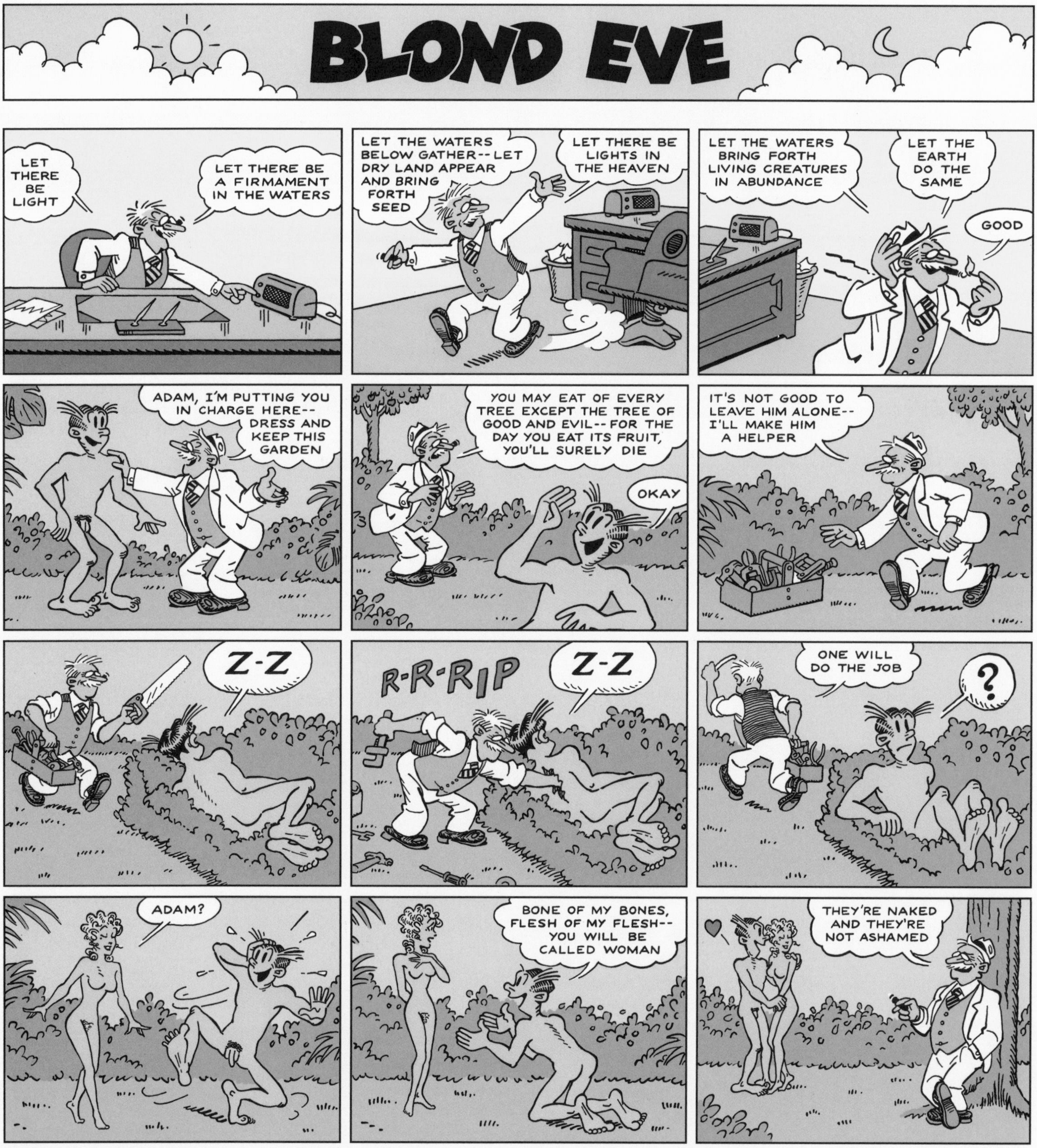
BLOND EVE
LET THERE BE LIGHT
LET THERE BE A FIRMAMENT IN THE WATERS
LET THE WATERS BELOW GATHER--LET DRY LAND APPEAR AND BRING FORTH SEED
LET THERE BE LIGHTS IN THE HEAVEN
LET THE WATERS BRING FORTH LIVING CREATURES IN ABUNDANCE
LET THE EARTH DO THE SAME
GOOD
ADAM, I'M PUTTING YOU IN CHARGE HERE-- DRESS AND KEEP THIS GARDEN
YOU MAY EAT OF EVERY TREE EXCEPT THE TREE OF GOOD AND EVIL--FOR THE DAY YOU EAT ITS FRUIT, YOU'LL SURELY DIE
OKAY
IT'S NOT GOOD TO LEAVE HIM ALONE-- I'LL MAKE HIM A HELPER
Z-Z
R-R-RIP
Z-Z
ONE WILL DO THE JOB
?
ADAM?
BONE OF MY BONES, FLESH OF MY FLESH-- YOU WILL BE CALLED WOMAN
THEY'RE NAKED AND THEY'RE NOT ASHAMED

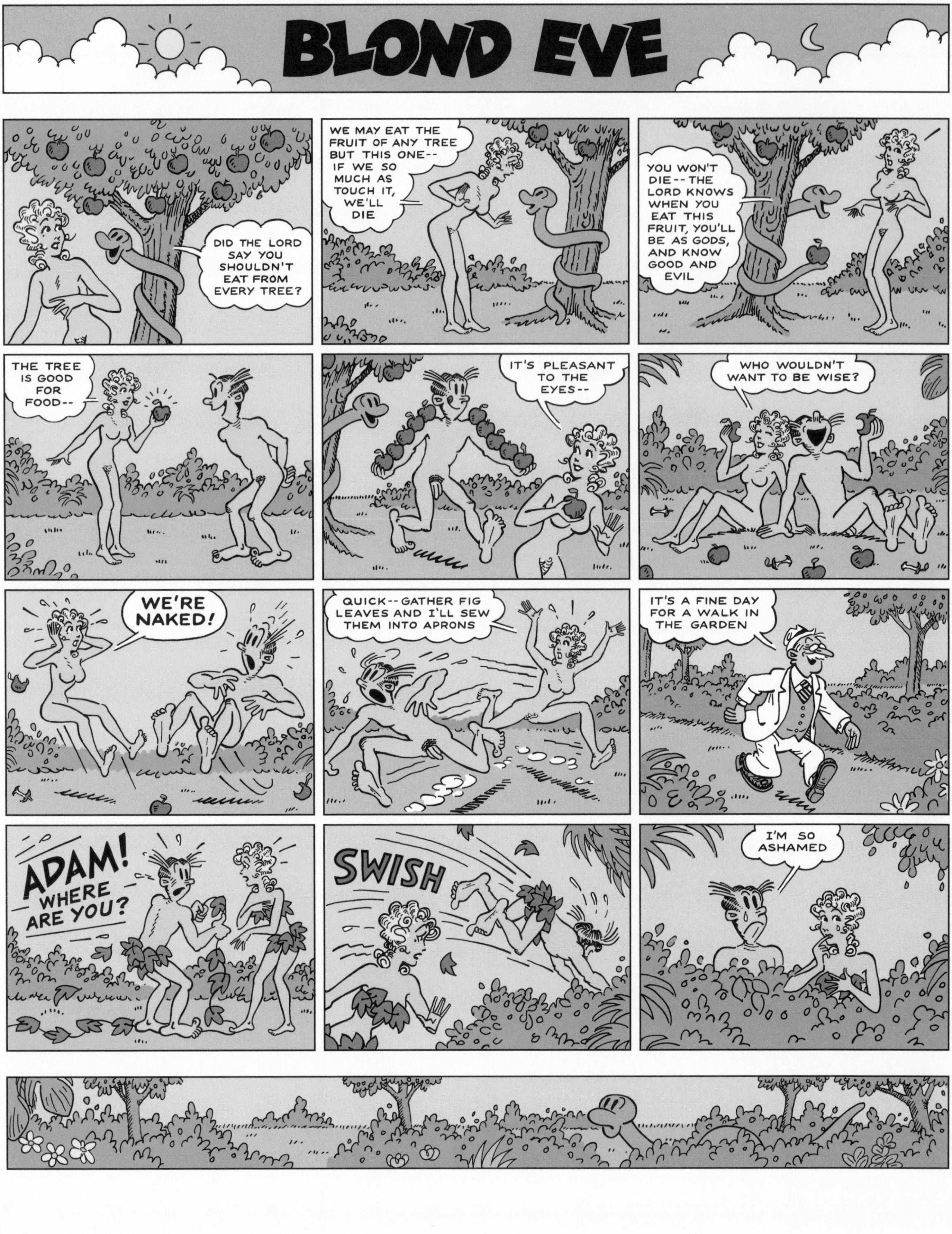
BLOND EVE
DID THE LORD SAY YOU SHOULDN'T EAT FROM EVERY TREE?
WE MAY EAT THE FRUIT OF ANY TREE BUT THIS ONE-- IF WE SO MUCH AS TOUCH IT, WE'LL DIE
YOU WON'T DIE-- THE LORD KNOWS WHEN YOU EAT THIS FRUIT, YOU'LL BE AS GODS, AND KNOW GOOD AND EVIL
THE TREE IS GOOD FOR FOOD--
IT'S PLEASANT TO THE EYES--
WHO WOULDN'T WANT TO BE WISE?
WE'RE NAKED!
QUICK-- GATHER FIG LEAVES AND I'LL SEW THEM INTO APRONS
IT'S A FINE DAY FOR A WALK IN THE GARDEN
ADAM! WHERE ARE YOU?
SWISH
I'M SO ASHAMED

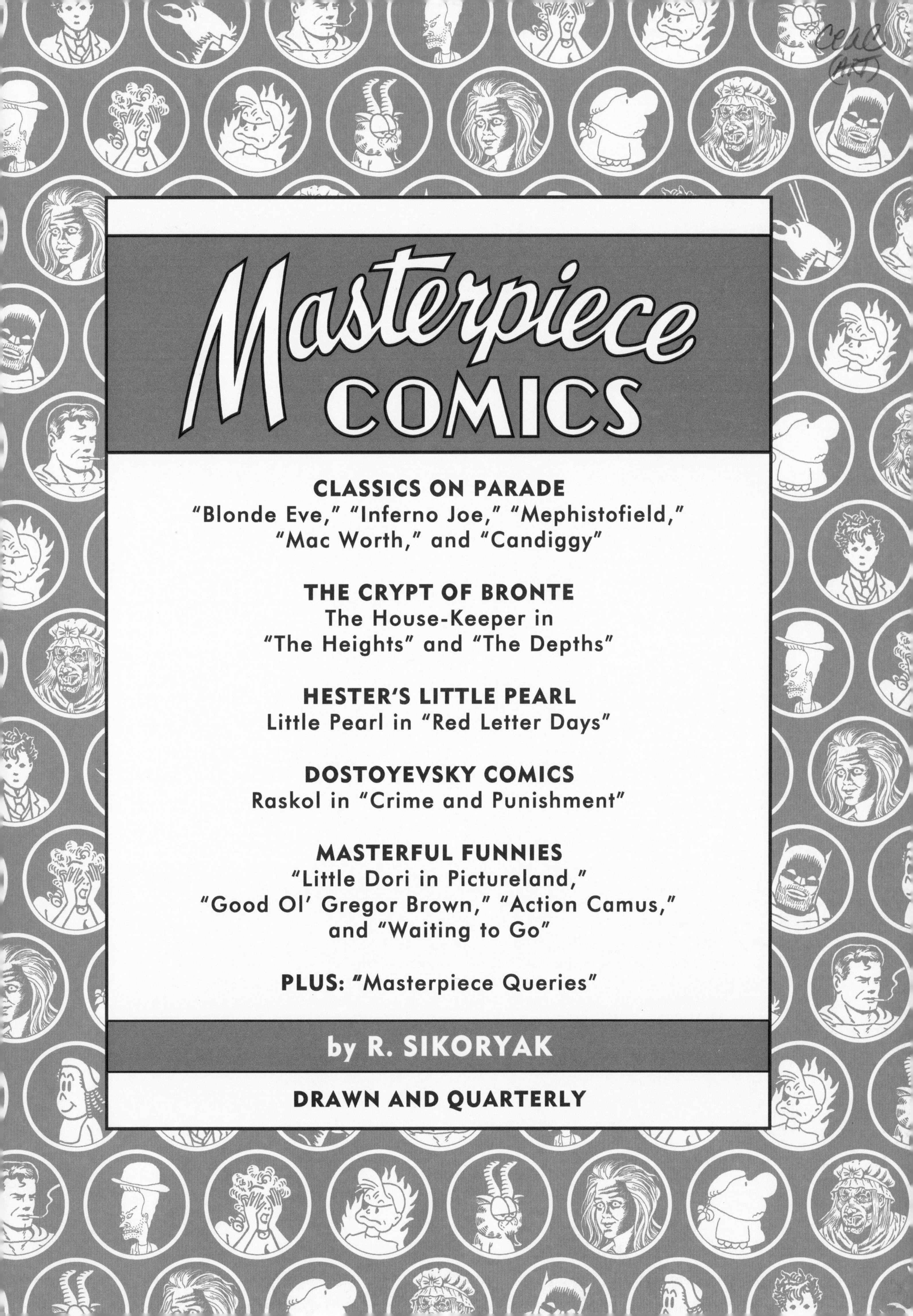

Masterpiece COMICS

CLASSICS ON PARADE
"Blonde Eve," "Inferno Joe," "Mephistofield,"
"Mac Worth," and "Candiggy"

THE CRYPT OF BRONTE
The House-Keeper in
"The Heights" and "The Depths"

HESTER'S LITTLE PEARL
Little Pearl in "Red Letter Days"

DOSTOYEVSKY COMICS
Raskol in "Crime and Punishment"

MASTERFUL FUNNIES
"Little Dori in Pictureland,"
"Good Ol' Gregor Brown," "Action Camus,"
and "Waiting to Go"

PLUS: "Masterpiece Queries"

by R. SIKORYAK

DRAWN AND QUARTERLY

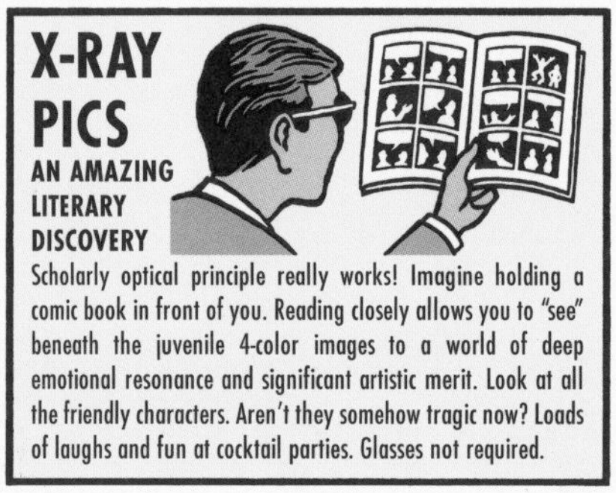
X-RAY
PICS
AN AMAZING
LITERARY
DISCOVERY
Scholarly optical principle really works! Imagine holding a comic book in front of you. Reading closely allows you to "see" beneath the juvenile 4-color images to a world of deep emotional resonance and significant artistic merit. Look at all the friendly characters. Aren't they somehow tragic now? Loads of laughs and fun at cocktail parties. Glasses not required.

For Kriota

Some of these stories were originally published in *Raw, Snake Eyes, New York Press, Monkeysuit, Reveal, Hotwire,* and *Drawn & Quarterly.*

Drawn & Quarterly
Post Office Box 48056
Montreal, Quebec
Canada H2V 4S8
www.drawnandquarterly.com

First edition: August 2009. Second printing: September 2009. Third printing: December 2009.
Fourth printing: April 2010.
Printed in Singapore.
10 9 8 7 6 5 4

Library and Archives Canada Cataloguing in Publication
Sikoryak, R.
Masterpiece Comics / by R. Sikoryak.
ISBN 978-1-897299-84-5
I. Title.
PN6727.S446M38 2009 741.5'973 C2009-900532-8

Distributed in the USA by:
Farrar, Straus and Giroux
18 West 18th Street
New York, NY 10011
Orders: 888.330.8477

Distributed in Canada by:
Raincoast Books
9050 Shaughnessy Street
Vancouver, BC V6P 6E5
Orders: 800.663.5714

Special thanks to my original editors: Art Spiegelman and Françoise Mouly; Glenn Head and Kaz; Michael Gentile; Mike Foran, Pat Giles, Chris McCulloch, and Miguel Martinez-Joffre; Scott Allie; Paul Karasik and Mark Newgarden; and Chris Oliveros.

Thanks also to Joe and Ellie Sikoryak, Joe Sikoryak, Steve Sikoryak, Todd Alcott, Steve Bissette, Charles Brownstein, Peggy Burns, Tom Daly, Tom Devlin, Chris Duffy, Bill Kartalopoulos, Jason Little, Diana Schutz, James Sturm, Kriota Willberg, Jaime Wolf... and everyone who's offered encouragement and support over the years.

With great acknowledgment (and sincere apologies) to:
Chic Young and Jim Raymond; Wesley Morse; Jim Davis; Allen Saunders and Ken Ernst; Nicholas P. Dallis, Marvin Bradley, and Frank Edgington; Tom Wilson; Al Feldstein and Jack Davis; Marjorie Henderson Buell, John Stanley, and Irving Tripp; Bob Kane, Bill Finger, Jerry Robinson, and Dick Sprang; Winsor McCay; Charles M. Schulz; Jerry Siegel, Joe Shuster, Wayne Boring, and Fred Ray; and Mike Judge.

Additional inspiration: Gustave Doré, Fritz Eichenberg, Francisco Goya, Rockwell Kent, Jean-Michel Moreau, and Louis Zansky.

The *Masterpiece Comics* project was supported in part by an Artists' Fellowship from the New York Foundation for the Arts (NYFA) and a Creative and Performing Artists and Writers Fellowship from the American Antiquarian Society.

No. 1

July

CLASSICS ON PARADE

10¢

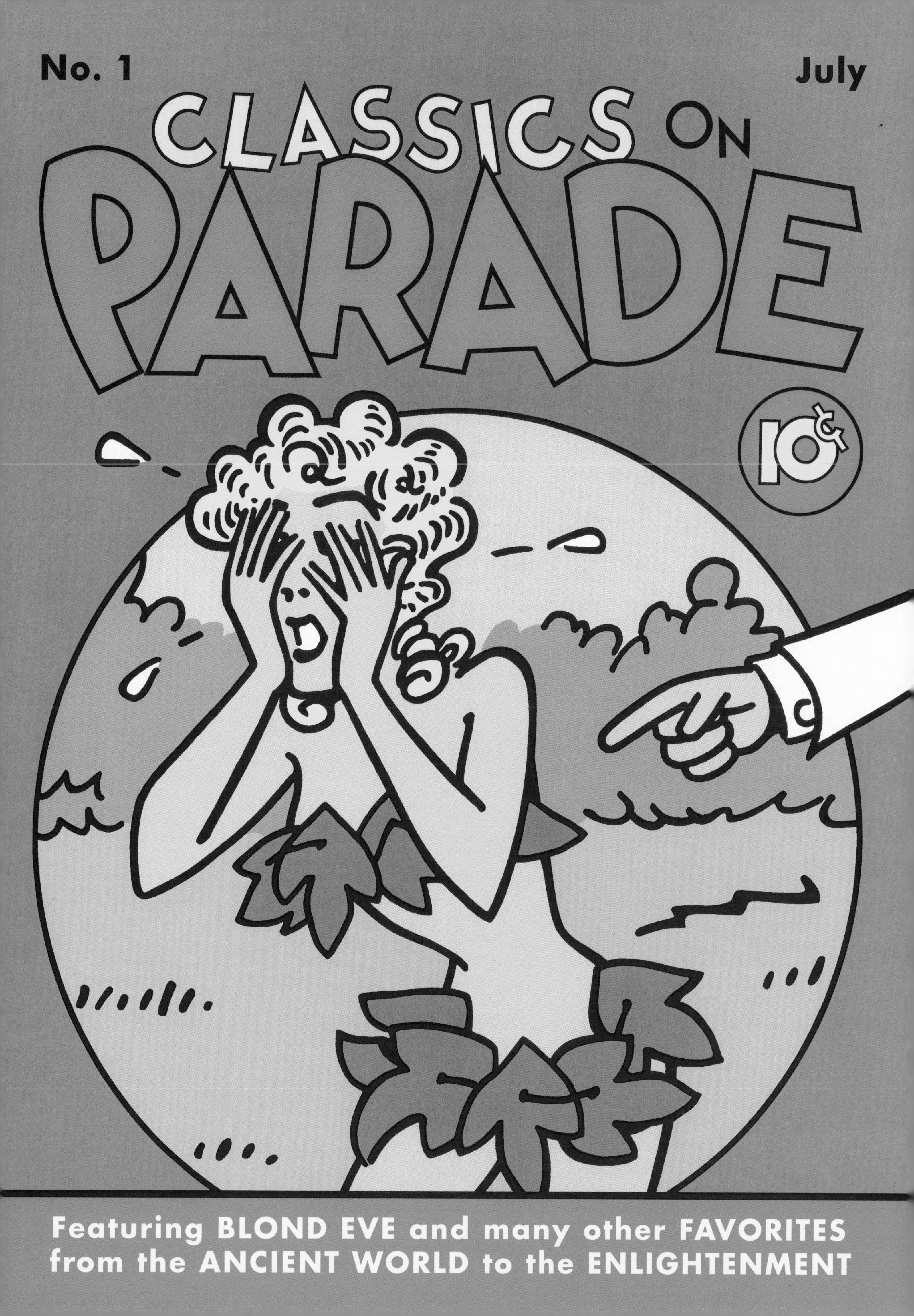

Featuring BLOND EVE and many other FAVORITES from the ANCIENT WORLD to the ENLIGHTENMENT

ADVERTISEMENT

DRAW HOMER!

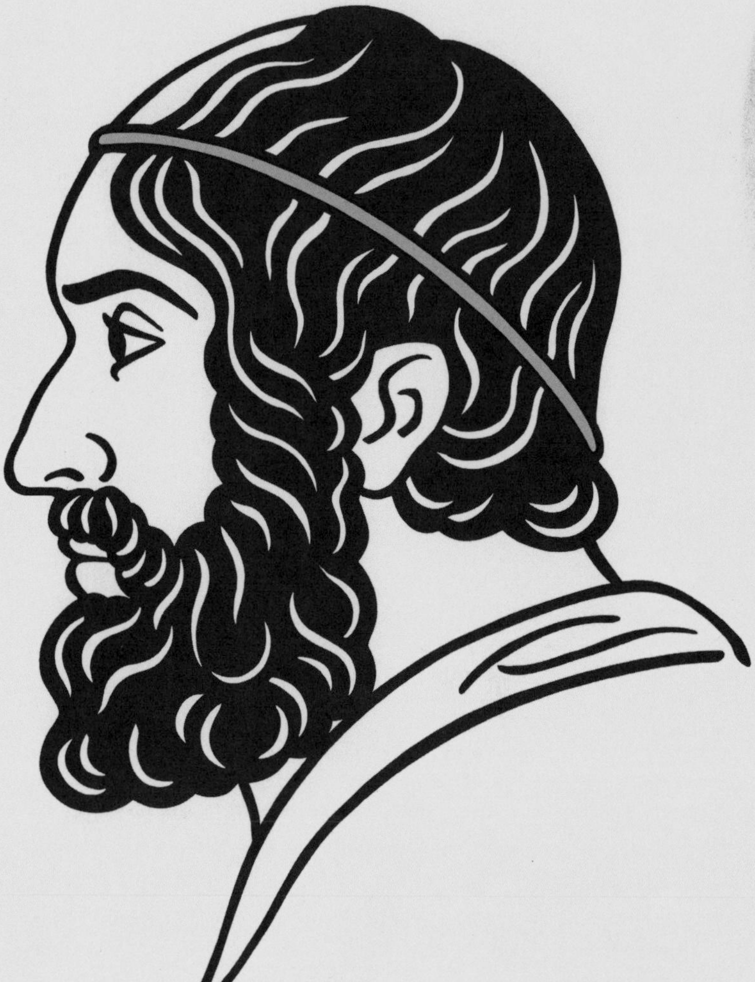

Try For A Free Literature Course!

5 PRIZES! 5 Complete Literature Courses, including Academic Gowns!

Draw the poet and try for a prize! Find out if you have profitable literary talent. You've nothing to lose -- *everything to gain.* Mail your drawing today!

Amateurs Only! Our students not eligible. Make a copy of poet 7 ins. high. Pencil or pen only. Omit lettering. All drawings must be received in 30 days. None returned. Winners notified.

BONUS FOR PROMPTNESS!

Mail drawing in next 5 days — we'll send you valuable folder on How to Read 4,000 Years of Literature — FREE!

LIT INSTRUCTION, INC., Dept. MC1, NY

Please enter my attached drawing in your literature contest.

(PLEASE PRINT)

Name ______________________ Age ______

Address ______________________ Phone ______

City ______________ Zone ______ Country ______

State ______________ Aspiration ______________

BLOND EVE
LORD, WE WERE AFRAID BECAUSE WE'RE NAKED
WHO TOLD YOU THAT YOU'RE NAKED? DID YOU EAT THE FRUIT OF THE FORBIDDEN TREE?
THE WOMAN GAVE IT TO ME
WHAT HAVE YOU DONE?
THE SERPENT TRICKED ME
BECAUSE YOU'VE DONE THIS, YOU ARE CURSED ABOVE EVERY BEAST! ON YOUR BELLY WILL YOU GO AND DUST WILL YOU EAT ALL THE DAYS OF YOUR LIFE!
WOMAN, I WILL MULTIPLY YOUR SORROW AND CONCEPTION! YOUR DESIRE WILL BE TO YOUR HUSBAND!
BECAUSE YOU'VE EATEN OF THE FORBIDDEN FRUIT, CURSED IS THE GROUND FOR YOUR SAKE
THORNS AND THISTLES WILL IT BRING YOU-- IN THE SWEAT OF YOUR BROW WILL YOU EAT BREAD, UNTIL YOU RETURN TO THE GROUND
FOR DUST YOU ARE, AND TO DUST YOU WILL RETURN
NOW, PUT ON SOME CLOTHES
LOOK, THE MAN IS AS ONE OF US, TO KNOW GOOD AND EVIL
NOW, GO AND TILL THE GROUND FROM WHICH YOU CAME
BOO HOO HOO
SIK OR YAK

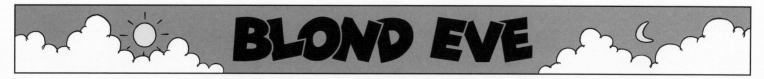

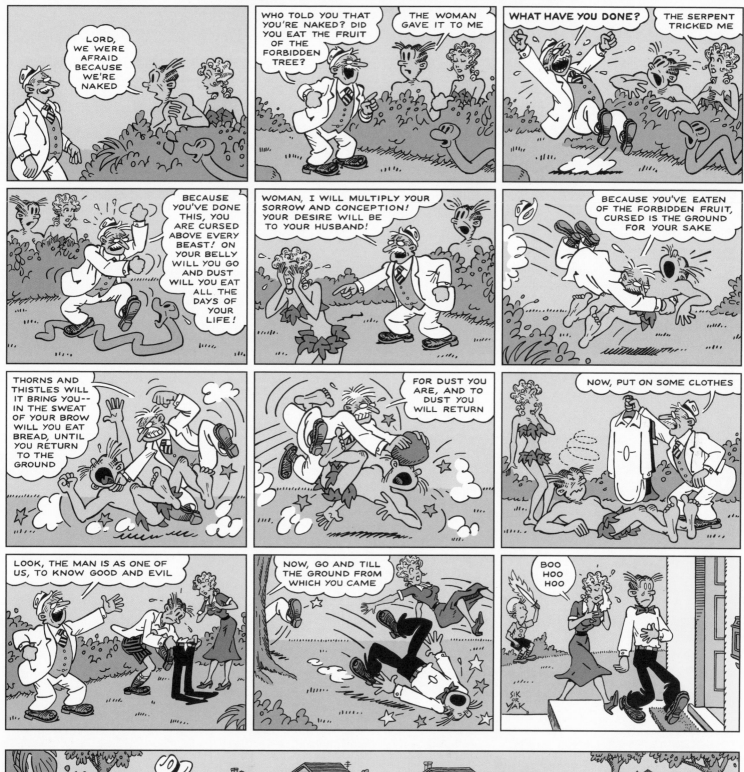

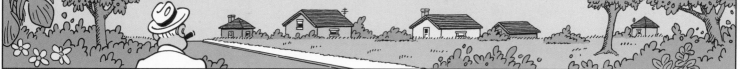

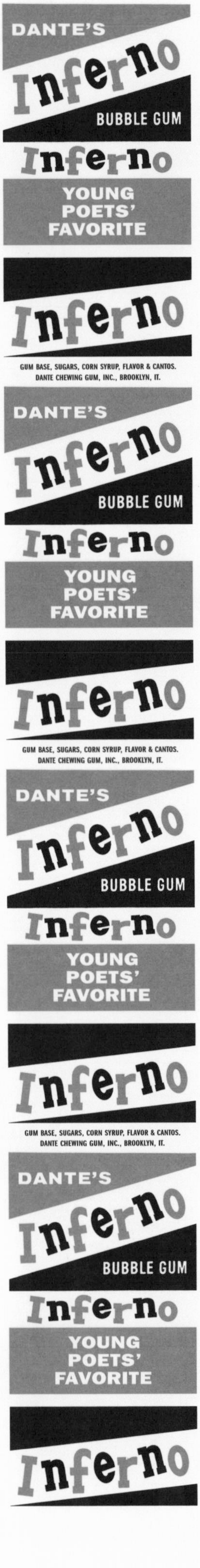
DANTE'S
Inferno
BUBBLE GUM
Inferno
YOUNG POETS' FAVORITE
Inferno
GUM BASE, SUGARS, CORN SYRUP, FLAVOR & CANTOS.
DANTE CHEWING GUM, INC., BROOKLYN, IT.

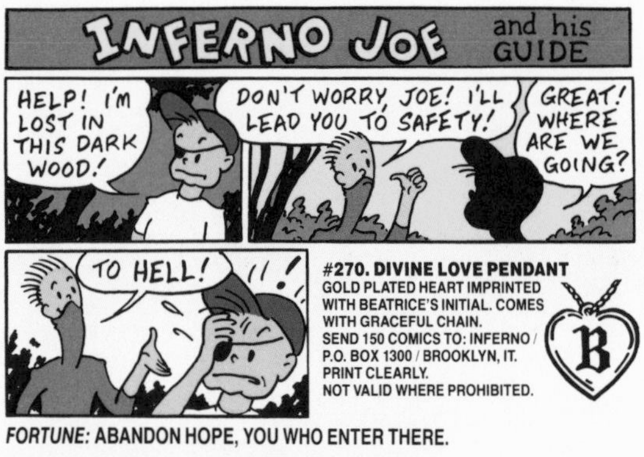
INFERNO JOE and his GUIDE
HELP! I'M LOST IN THIS DARK WOOD!
DON'T WORRY, JOE! I'LL LEAD YOU TO SAFETY!
GREAT! WHERE ARE WE GOING?
TO HELL!
#270. DIVINE LOVE PENDANT
GOLD PLATED HEART IMPRINTED WITH BEATRICE'S INITIAL. COMES WITH GRACEFUL CHAIN. SEND 150 COMICS TO: INFERNO / P.O. BOX 1300 / BROOKLYN, IT. PRINT CLEARLY. NOT VALID WHERE PROHIBITED.
B
FORTUNE: ABANDON HOPE, YOU WHO ENTER THERE.

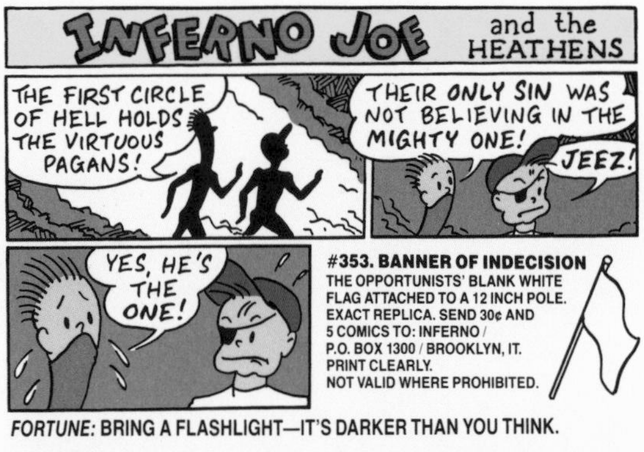
INFERNO JOE and the HEATHENS
THE FIRST CIRCLE OF HELL HOLDS THE VIRTUOUS PAGANS!
THEIR ONLY SIN WAS NOT BELIEVING IN THE MIGHTY ONE!
JEEZ!
YES, HE'S THE ONE!
#353. BANNER OF INDECISION
THE OPPORTUNISTS' BLANK WHITE FLAG ATTACHED TO A 12 INCH POLE. EXACT REPLICA. SEND 30¢ AND 5 COMICS TO: INFERNO / P.O. BOX 1300 / BROOKLYN, IT. PRINT CLEARLY. NOT VALID WHERE PROHIBITED.
FORTUNE: BRING A FLASHLIGHT—IT'S DARKER THAN YOU THINK.

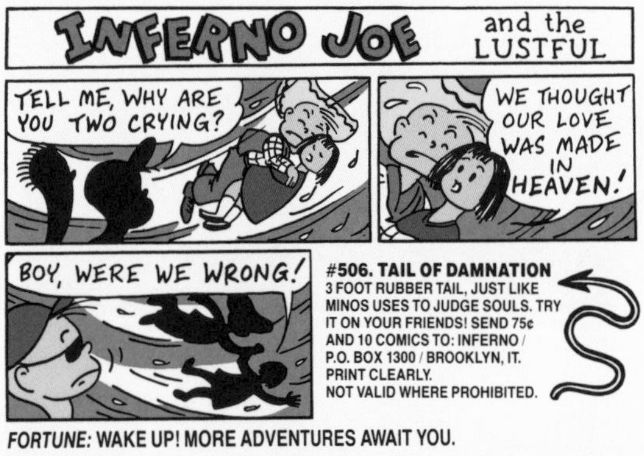
INFERNO JOE and the LUSTFUL
TELL ME, WHY ARE YOU TWO CRYING?
WE THOUGHT OUR LOVE WAS MADE IN HEAVEN!
BOY, WERE WE WRONG!
#506. TAIL OF DAMNATION
3 FOOT RUBBER TAIL, JUST LIKE MINOS USES TO JUDGE SOULS. TRY IT ON YOUR FRIENDS! SEND 75¢ AND 10 COMICS TO: INFERNO / P.O. BOX 1300 / BROOKLYN, IT. PRINT CLEARLY. NOT VALID WHERE PROHIBITED.
FORTUNE: WAKE UP! MORE ADVENTURES AWAIT YOU.

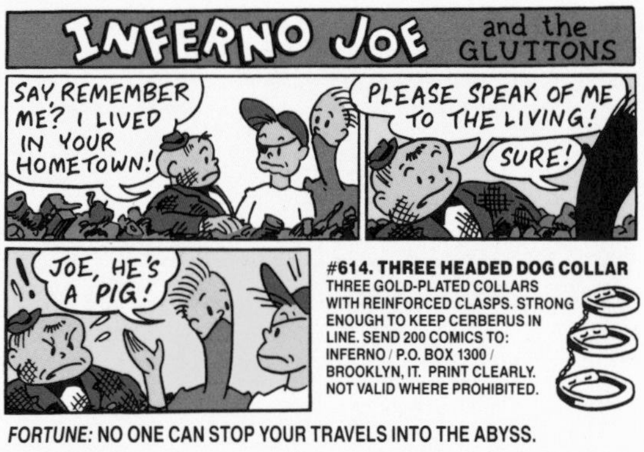
INFERNO JOE and the GLUTTONS
SAY, REMEMBER ME? I LIVED IN YOUR HOMETOWN!
PLEASE SPEAK OF ME TO THE LIVING!
SURE!
JOE, HE'S A PIG!
#614. THREE HEADED DOG COLLAR
THREE GOLD-PLATED COLLARS WITH REINFORCED CLASPS. STRONG ENOUGH TO KEEP CERBERUS IN LINE. SEND 200 COMICS TO: INFERNO / P.O. BOX 1300 / BROOKLYN, IT. PRINT CLEARLY. NOT VALID WHERE PROHIBITED.
FORTUNE: NO ONE CAN STOP YOUR TRAVELS INTO THE ABYSS.

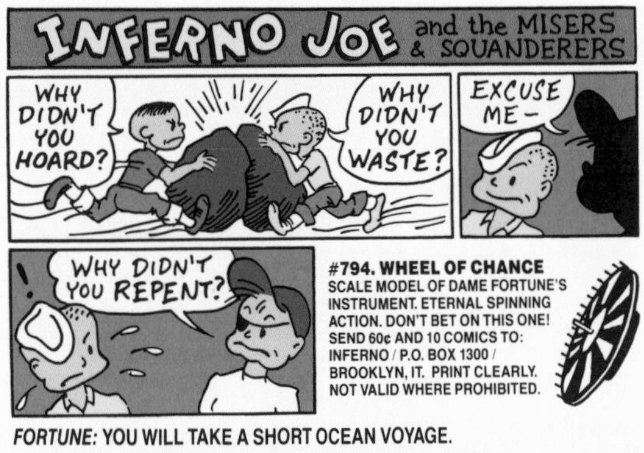
INFERNO JOE and the MISERS & SQUANDERERS
WHY DIDN'T YOU HOARD?
WHY DIDN'T YOU WASTE?
EXCUSE ME—
WHY DIDN'T YOU REPENT?
#794. WHEEL OF CHANCE
SCALE MODEL OF DAME FORTUNE'S INSTRUMENT. ETERNAL SPINNING ACTION. DON'T BET ON THIS ONE! SEND 60¢ AND 10 COMICS TO: INFERNO / P.O. BOX 1300 / BROOKLYN, IT. PRINT CLEARLY. NOT VALID WHERE PROHIBITED.
FORTUNE: YOU WILL TAKE A SHORT OCEAN VOYAGE.

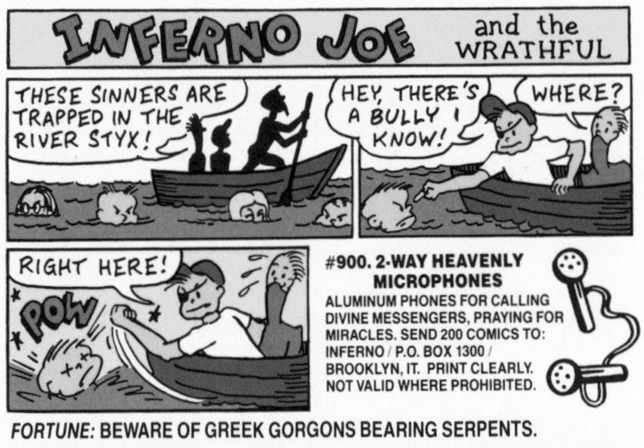
INFERNO JOE and the WRATHFUL
THESE SINNERS ARE TRAPPED IN THE RIVER STYX!
HEY, THERE'S A BULLY I KNOW!
WHERE?
RIGHT HERE!
POW
#900. 2-WAY HEAVENLY MICROPHONES
ALUMINUM PHONES FOR CALLING DIVINE MESSENGERS, PRAYING FOR MIRACLES. SEND 200 COMICS TO: INFERNO / P.O. BOX 1300 / BROOKLYN, IT. PRINT CLEARLY. NOT VALID WHERE PROHIBITED.
FORTUNE: BEWARE OF GREEK GORGONS BEARING SERPENTS.

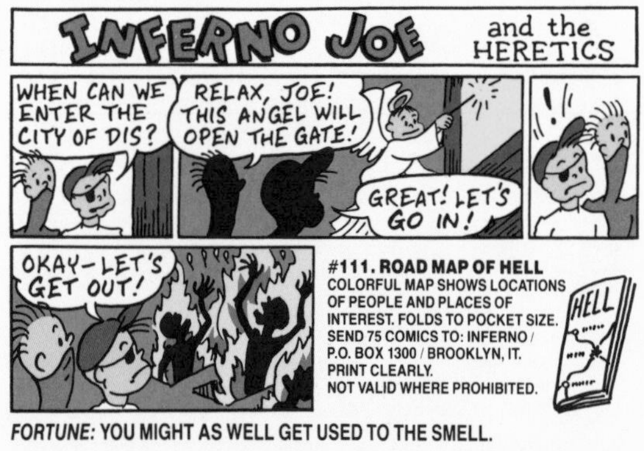
INFERNO JOE and the HERETICS
WHEN CAN WE ENTER THE CITY OF DIS?
RELAX, JOE! THIS ANGEL WILL OPEN THE GATE!
GREAT! LET'S GO IN!
OKAY—LET'S GET OUT!
#111. ROAD MAP OF HELL
COLORFUL MAP SHOWS LOCATIONS OF PEOPLE AND PLACES OF INTEREST. FOLDS TO POCKET SIZE. SEND 75 COMICS TO: INFERNO / P.O. BOX 1300 / BROOKLYN, IT. PRINT CLEARLY. NOT VALID WHERE PROHIBITED.
HELL
FORTUNE: YOU MIGHT AS WELL GET USED TO THE SMELL.

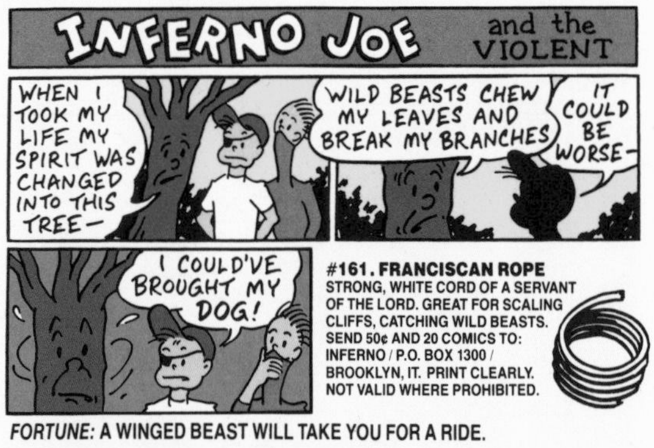
INFERNO JOE and the VIOLENT
WHEN I TOOK MY LIFE MY SPIRIT WAS CHANGED INTO THIS TREE—
WILD BEASTS CHEW MY LEAVES AND BREAK MY BRANCHES!
IT COULD BE WORSE—
I COULD'VE BROUGHT MY DOG!
#161. FRANCISCAN ROPE
STRONG, WHITE CORD OF A SERVANT OF THE LORD. GREAT FOR SCALING CLIFFS, CATCHING WILD BEASTS. SEND 50¢ AND 20 COMICS TO: INFERNO / P.O. BOX 1300 / BROOKLYN, IT. PRINT CLEARLY. NOT VALID WHERE PROHIBITED.
FORTUNE: A WINGED BEAST WILL TAKE YOU FOR A RIDE.

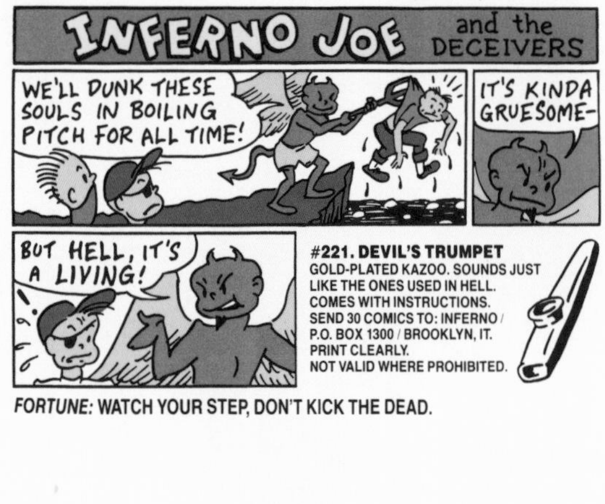
INFERNO JOE and the DECEIVERS
WE'LL DUNK THESE SOULS IN BOILING PITCH FOR ALL TIME!
IT'S KINDA GRUESOME—
BUT HELL, IT'S A LIVING!
#221. DEVIL'S TRUMPET
GOLD-PLATED KAZOO. SOUNDS JUST LIKE THE ONES USED IN HELL. COMES WITH INSTRUCTIONS. SEND 30 COMICS TO: INFERNO / P.O. BOX 1300 / BROOKLYN, IT. PRINT CLEARLY. NOT VALID WHERE PROHIBITED.
FORTUNE: WATCH YOUR STEP, DON'T KICK THE DEAD.

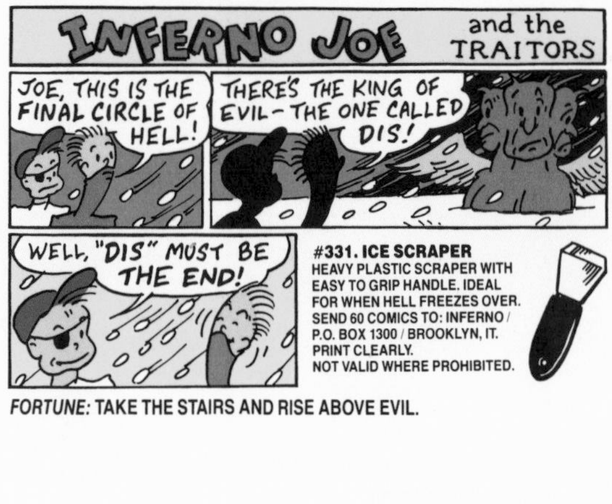
INFERNO JOE and the TRAITORS
JOE, THIS IS THE FINAL CIRCLE OF HELL!
THERE'S THE KING OF EVIL—THE ONE CALLED DIS!
WELL, "DIS" MUST BE THE END!
#331. ICE SCRAPER
HEAVY PLASTIC SCRAPER WITH EASY TO GRIP HANDLE. IDEAL FOR WHEN HELL FREEZES OVER. SEND 60 COMICS TO: INFERNO / P.O. BOX 1300 / BROOKLYN, IT. PRINT CLEARLY. NOT VALID WHERE PROHIBITED.
FORTUNE: TAKE THE STAIRS AND RISE ABOVE EVIL.

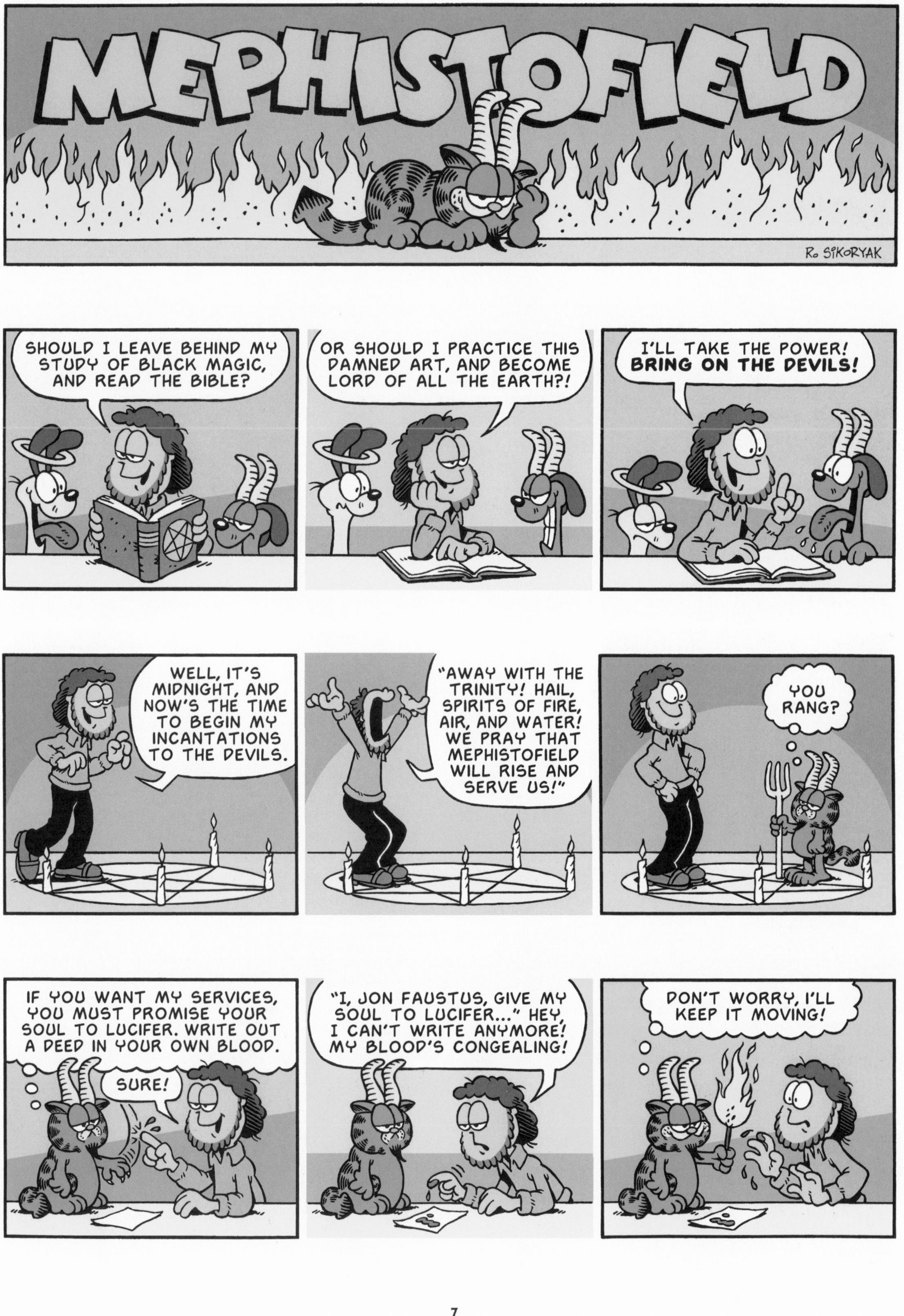
MEPHISTOFIELD
R. SIKORYAK
SHOULD I LEAVE BEHIND MY STUDY OF BLACK MAGIC, AND READ THE BIBLE?
OR SHOULD I PRACTICE THIS DAMNED ART, AND BECOME LORD OF ALL THE EARTH?!
I'LL TAKE THE POWER! **BRING ON THE DEVILS!**
WELL, IT'S MIDNIGHT, AND NOW'S THE TIME TO BEGIN MY INCANTATIONS TO THE DEVILS.
"AWAY WITH THE TRINITY! HAIL, SPIRITS OF FIRE, AIR, AND WATER! WE PRAY THAT MEPHISTOFIELD WILL RISE AND SERVE US!"
YOU RANG?
IF YOU WANT MY SERVICES, YOU MUST PROMISE YOUR SOUL TO LUCIFER. WRITE OUT A DEED IN YOUR OWN BLOOD.
SURE!
"I, JON FAUSTUS, GIVE MY SOUL TO LUCIFER..." HEY, I CAN'T WRITE ANYMORE! MY BLOOD'S CONGEALING!
DON'T WORRY, I'LL KEEP IT MOVING!

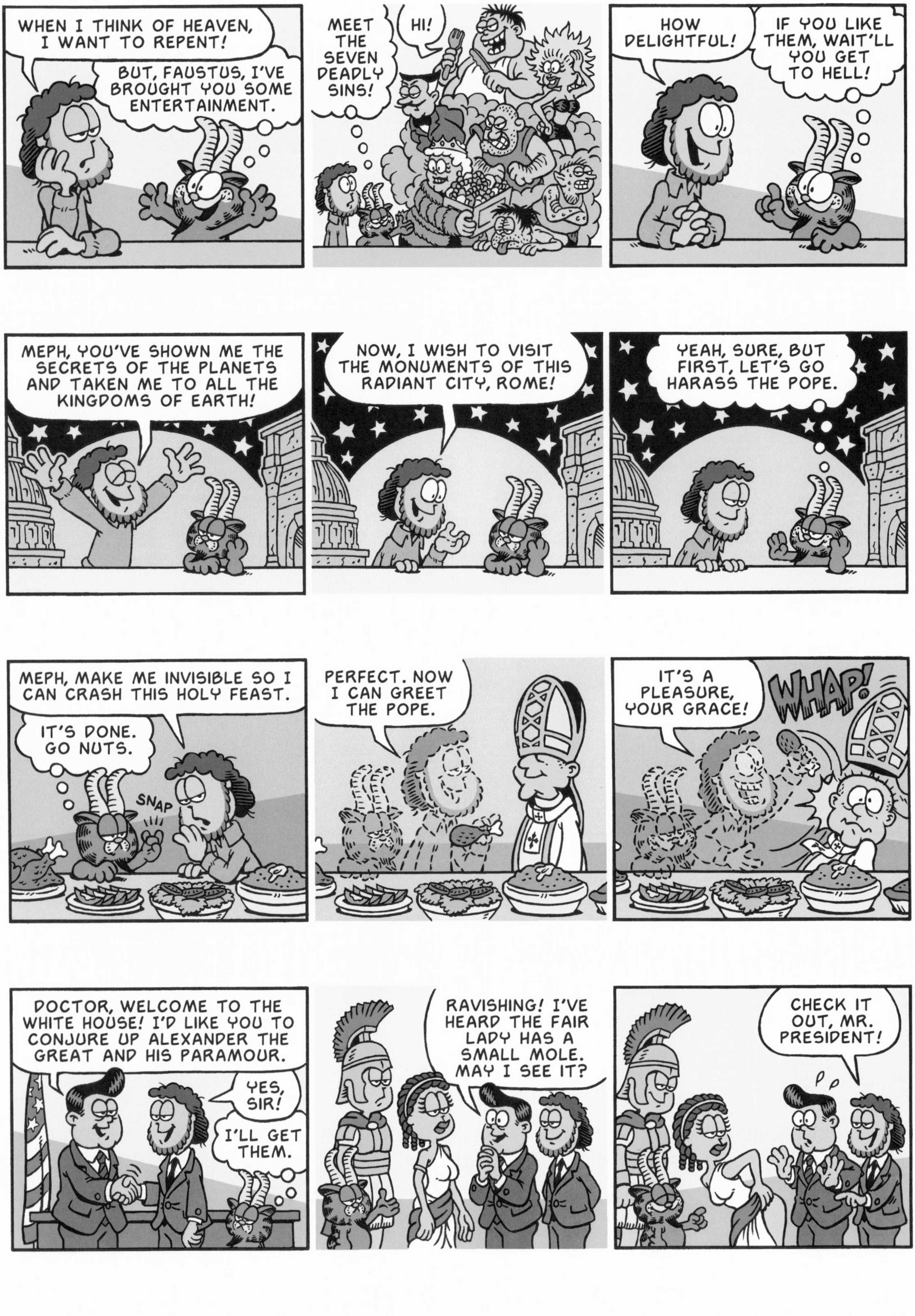
WHEN I THINK OF HEAVEN, I WANT TO REPENT!
BUT, FAUSTUS, I'VE BROUGHT YOU SOME ENTERTAINMENT.
MEET THE SEVEN DEADLY SINS!
HI!
HOW DELIGHTFUL!
IF YOU LIKE THEM, WAIT'LL YOU GET TO HELL!
MEPH, YOU'VE SHOWN ME THE SECRETS OF THE PLANETS AND TAKEN ME TO ALL THE KINGDOMS OF EARTH!
NOW, I WISH TO VISIT THE MONUMENTS OF THIS RADIANT CITY, ROME!
YEAH, SURE, BUT FIRST, LET'S GO HARASS THE POPE.
MEPH, MAKE ME INVISIBLE SO I CAN CRASH THIS HOLY FEAST.
IT'S DONE. GO NUTS.
SNAP
PERFECT. NOW I CAN GREET THE POPE.
IT'S A PLEASURE, YOUR GRACE!
WHAP!
DOCTOR, WELCOME TO THE WHITE HOUSE! I'D LIKE YOU TO CONJURE UP ALEXANDER THE GREAT AND HIS PARAMOUR.
YES, SIR!
I'LL GET THEM.
RAVISHING! I'VE HEARD THE FAIR LADY HAS A SMALL MOLE. MAY I SEE IT?
CHECK IT OUT, MR. PRESIDENT!

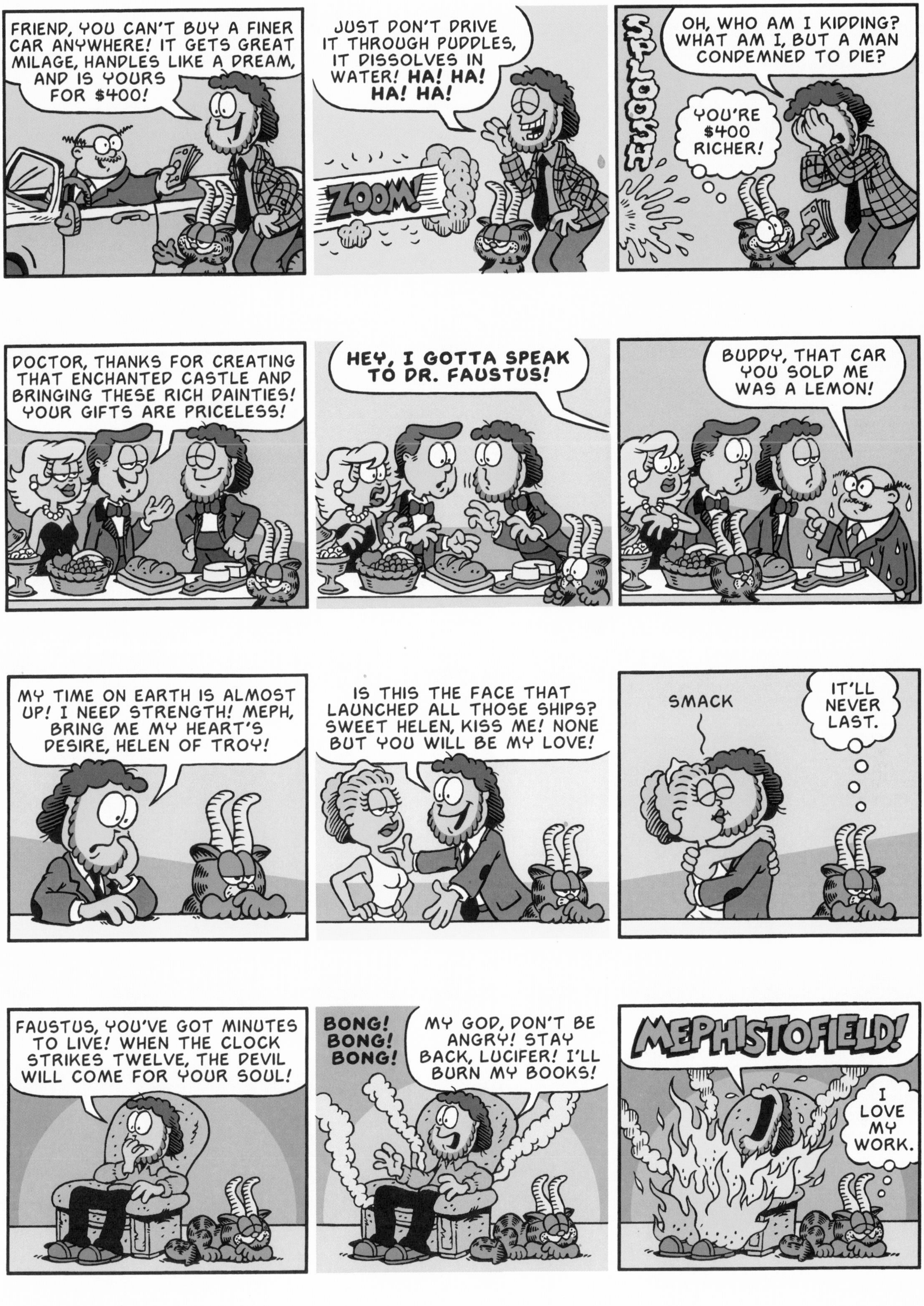
FRIEND, YOU CAN'T BUY A FINER CAR ANYWHERE! IT GETS GREAT MILAGE, HANDLES LIKE A DREAM, AND IS YOURS FOR $400!
JUST DON'T DRIVE IT THROUGH PUDDLES, IT DISSOLVES IN WATER! HA! HA! HA! HA!
ZOOM!
SPLOOSH
OH, WHO AM I KIDDING? WHAT AM I, BUT A MAN CONDEMNED TO DIE?
YOU'RE $400 RICHER!
DOCTOR, THANKS FOR CREATING THAT ENCHANTED CASTLE AND BRINGING THESE RICH DAINTIES! YOUR GIFTS ARE PRICELESS!
HEY, I GOTTA SPEAK TO DR. FAUSTUS!
BUDDY, THAT CAR YOU SOLD ME WAS A LEMON!
MY TIME ON EARTH IS ALMOST UP! I NEED STRENGTH! MEPH, BRING ME MY HEART'S DESIRE, HELEN OF TROY!
IS THIS THE FACE THAT LAUNCHED ALL THOSE SHIPS? SWEET HELEN, KISS ME! NONE BUT YOU WILL BE MY LOVE!
SMACK
IT'LL NEVER LAST.
FAUSTUS, YOU'VE GOT MINUTES TO LIVE! WHEN THE CLOCK STRIKES TWELVE, THE DEVIL WILL COME FOR YOUR SOUL!
BONG! BONG! BONG!
MY GOD, DON'T BE ANGRY! STAY BACK, LUCIFER! I'LL BURN MY BOOKS!
MEPHISTOFIELD!
I LOVE MY WORK.

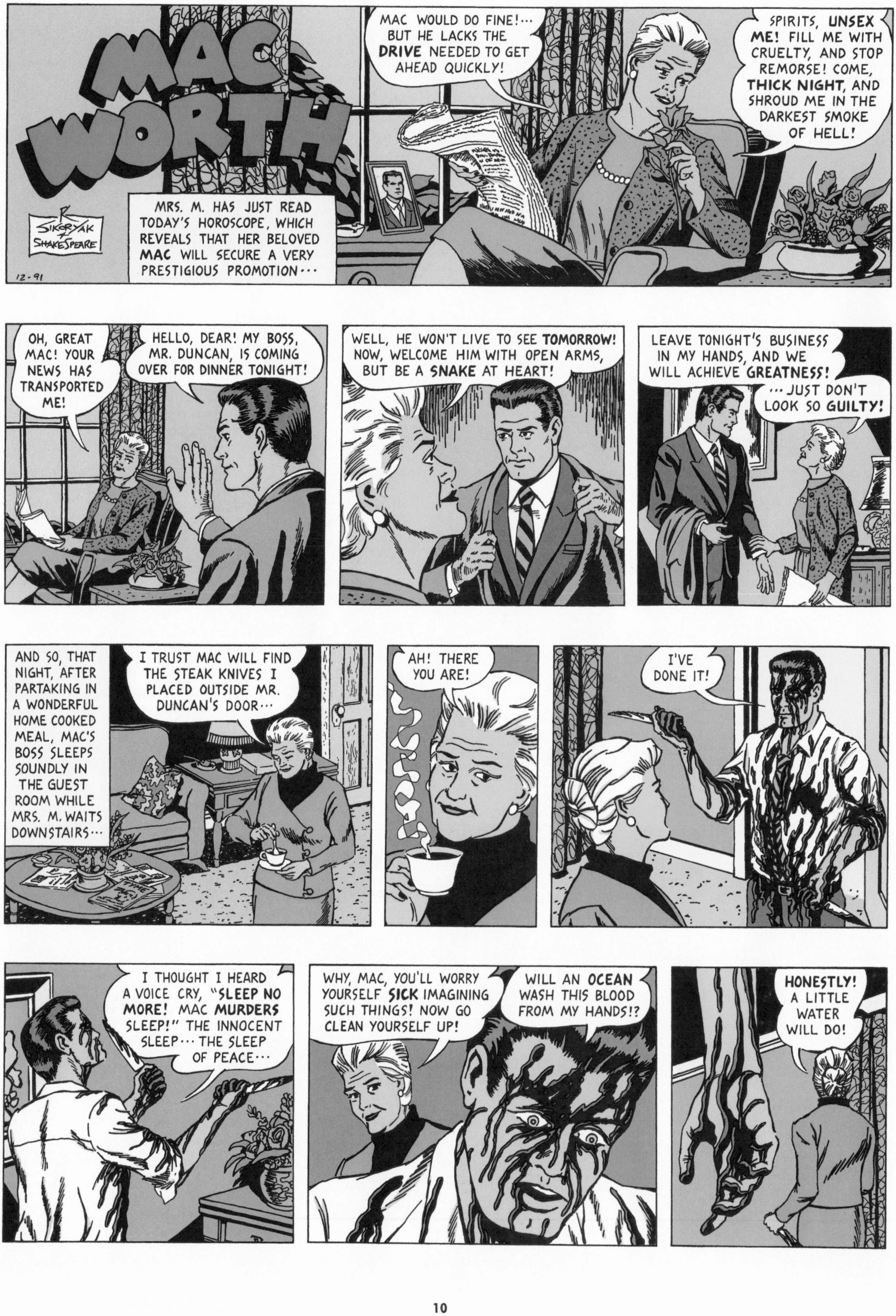
MAC WORTH
SIKORYAK & SHAKESPEARE
12-91
MRS. M. HAS JUST READ TODAY'S HOROSCOPE, WHICH REVEALS THAT HER BELOVED MAC WILL SECURE A VERY PRESTIGIOUS PROMOTION···
MAC WOULD DO FINE!··· BUT HE LACKS THE DRIVE NEEDED TO GET AHEAD QUICKLY!
SPIRITS, UNSEX ME! FILL ME WITH CRUELTY, AND STOP REMORSE! COME, THICK NIGHT, AND SHROUD ME IN THE DARKEST SMOKE OF HELL!
OH, GREAT MAC! YOUR NEWS HAS TRANSPORTED ME!
HELLO, DEAR! MY BOSS, MR. DUNCAN, IS COMING OVER FOR DINNER TONIGHT!
WELL, HE WON'T LIVE TO SEE TOMORROW! NOW, WELCOME HIM WITH OPEN ARMS, BUT BE A SNAKE AT HEART!
LEAVE TONIGHT'S BUSINESS IN MY HANDS, AND WE WILL ACHIEVE GREATNESS!
···JUST DON'T LOOK SO GUILTY!
AND SO, THAT NIGHT, AFTER PARTAKING IN A WONDERFUL HOME COOKED MEAL, MAC'S BOSS SLEEPS SOUNDLY IN THE GUEST ROOM WHILE MRS. M. WAITS DOWNSTAIRS···
I TRUST MAC WILL FIND THE STEAK KNIVES I PLACED OUTSIDE MR. DUNCAN'S DOOR···
AH! THERE YOU ARE!
I'VE DONE IT!
I THOUGHT I HEARD A VOICE CRY, "SLEEP NO MORE! MAC MURDERS SLEEP!" THE INNOCENT SLEEP··· THE SLEEP OF PEACE···
WHY, MAC, YOU'LL WORRY YOURSELF SICK IMAGINING SUCH THINGS! NOW GO CLEAN YOURSELF UP!
WILL AN OCEAN WASH THIS BLOOD FROM MY HANDS!?
HONESTLY! A LITTLE WATER WILL DO!

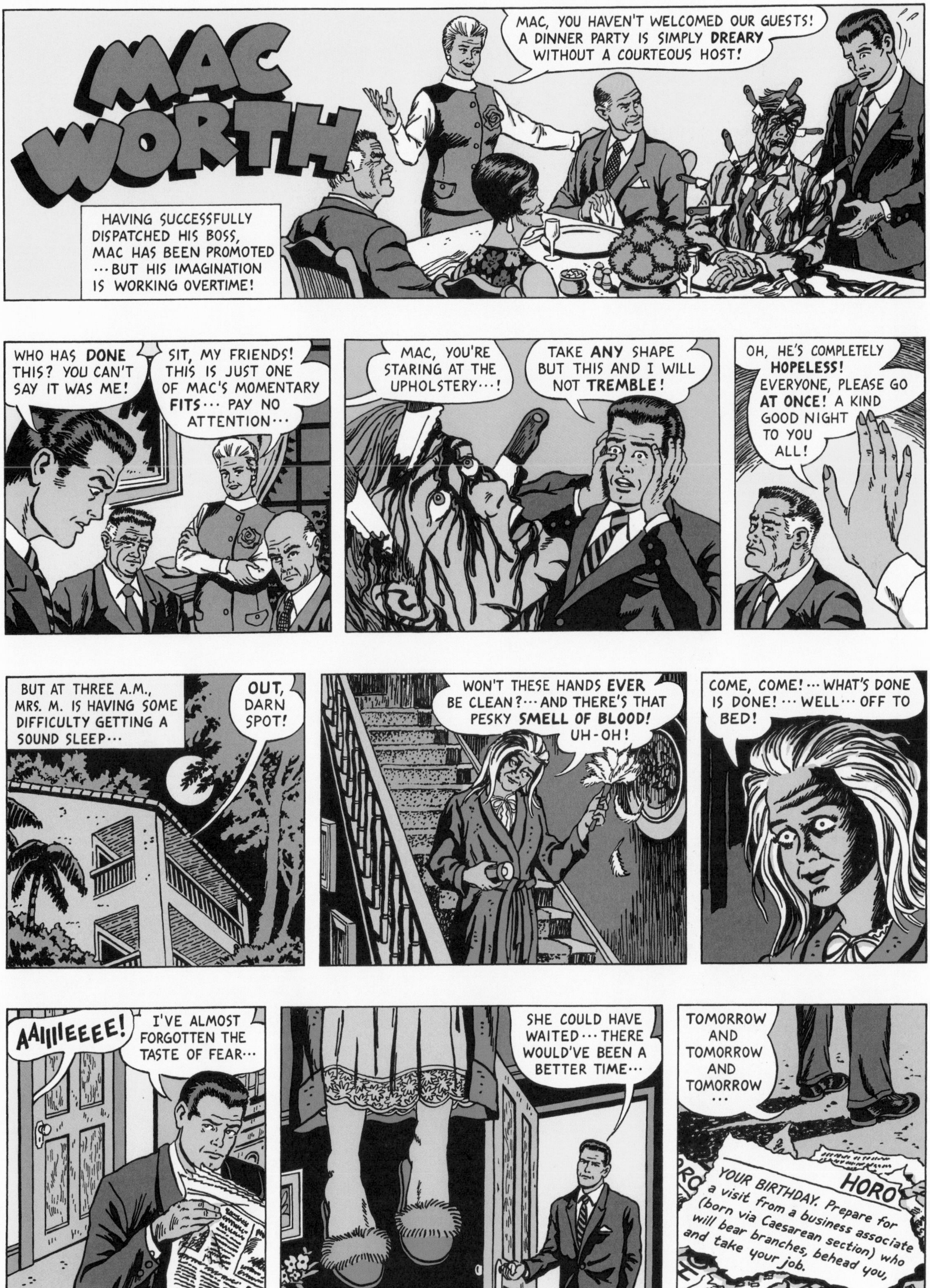
MAC WORTH
HAVING SUCCESSFULLY DISPATCHED HIS BOSS, MAC HAS BEEN PROMOTED ··· BUT HIS IMAGINATION IS WORKING OVERTIME!
MAC, YOU HAVEN'T WELCOMED OUR GUESTS! A DINNER PARTY IS SIMPLY DREARY WITHOUT A COURTEOUS HOST!
WHO HAS DONE THIS? YOU CAN'T SAY IT WAS ME!
SIT, MY FRIENDS! THIS IS JUST ONE OF MAC'S MOMENTARY FITS··· PAY NO ATTENTION···
MAC, YOU'RE STARING AT THE UPHOLSTERY···!
TAKE ANY SHAPE BUT THIS AND I WILL NOT TREMBLE!
OH, HE'S COMPLETELY HOPELESS! EVERYONE, PLEASE GO AT ONCE! A KIND GOOD NIGHT TO YOU ALL!
BUT AT THREE A.M., MRS. M. IS HAVING SOME DIFFICULTY GETTING A SOUND SLEEP···
OUT, DARN SPOT!
WON'T THESE HANDS EVER BE CLEAN?··· AND THERE'S THAT PESKY SMELL OF BLOOD! UH-OH!
COME, COME! ··· WHAT'S DONE IS DONE! ··· WELL··· OFF TO BED!
AAIIIEEEE!
I'VE ALMOST FORGOTTEN THE TASTE OF FEAR···
SHE COULD HAVE WAITED··· THERE WOULD'VE BEEN A BETTER TIME···
TOMORROW AND TOMORROW AND TOMORROW ···
HORO
YOUR BIRTHDAY. Prepare for a visit from a business associate (born via Caesarean section) who will bear branches, behead you, and take your job.

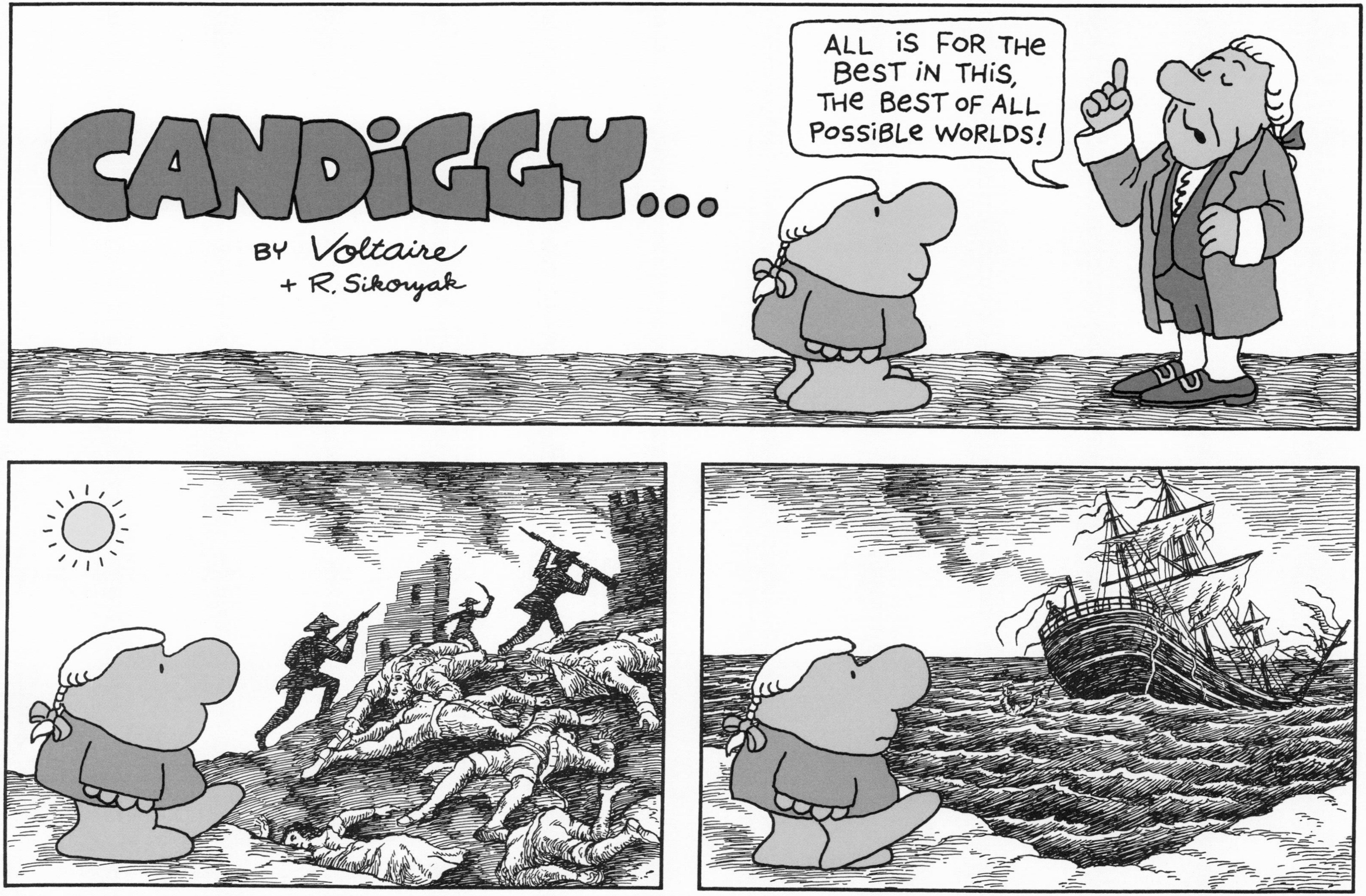
CANDiGGY...
BY Voltaire
+ R. Sikoryak
ALL is FOR THE BEST iN THiS, THe BEST OF ALL POSSiBLe WORLDS!

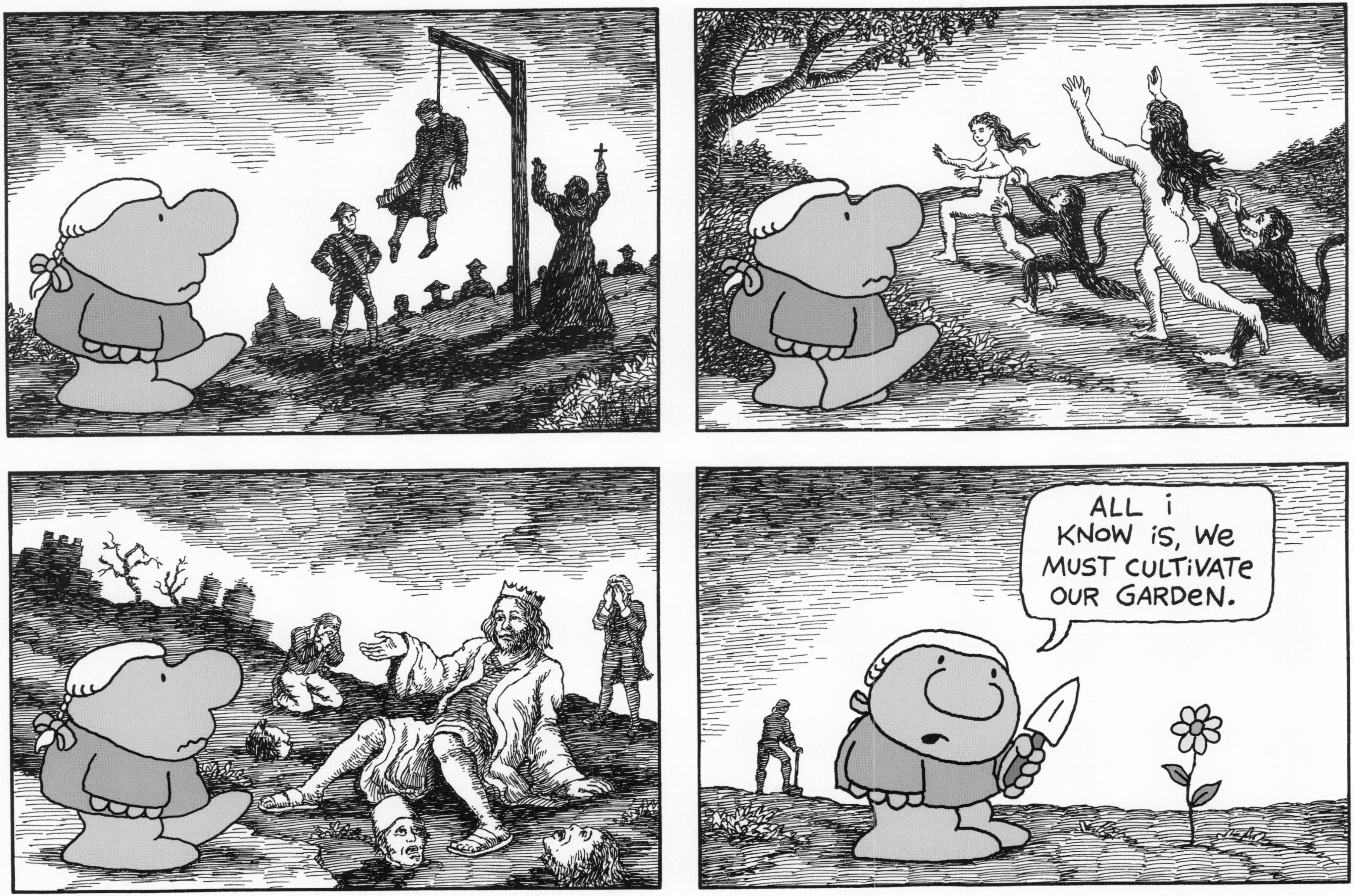
ALL i KNOW iS, We MUST CULTiVATe OUR GARDeN.

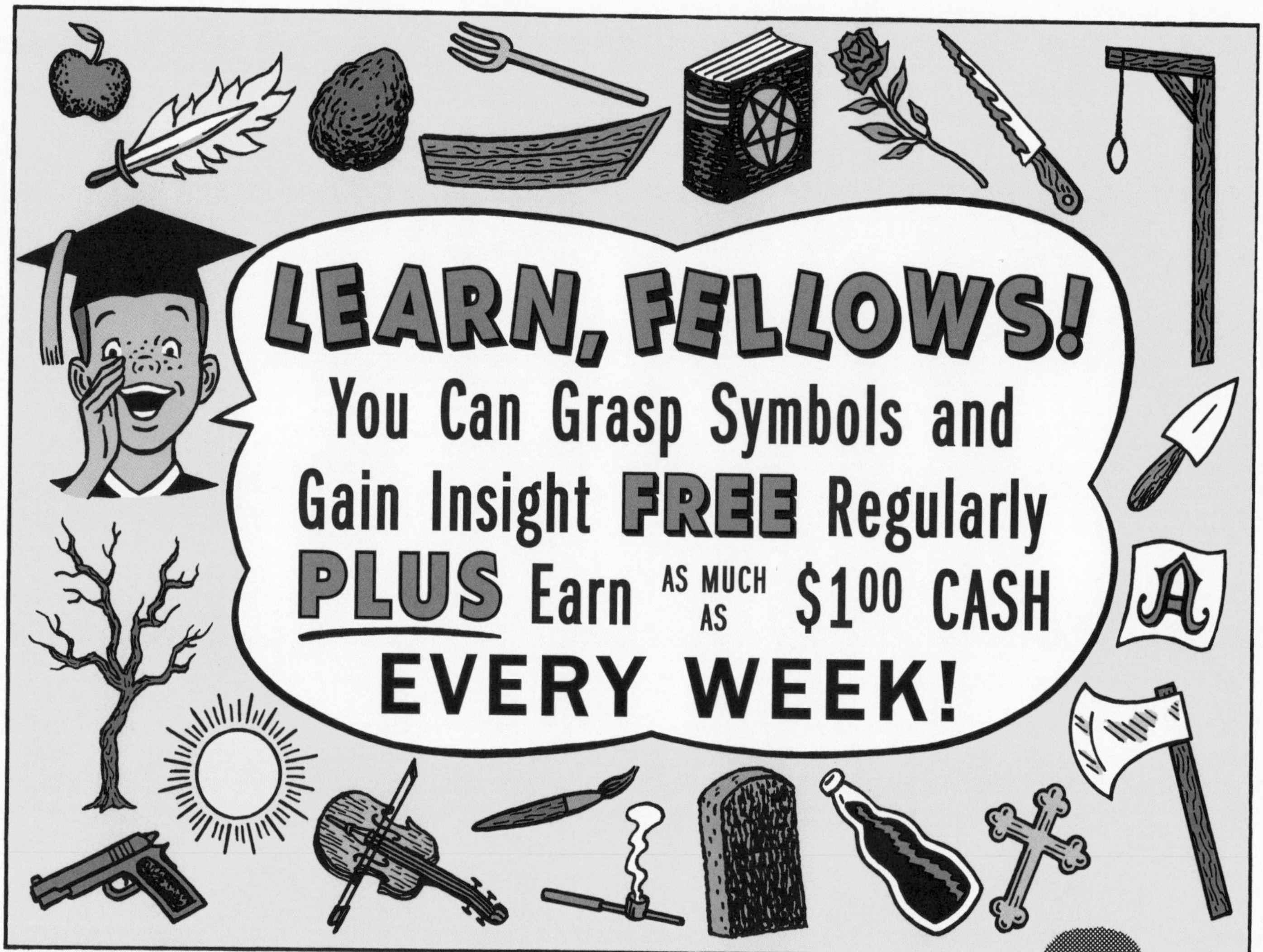
LEARN, FELLOWS!
You Can Grasp Symbols and
Gain Insight FREE Regularly
PLUS Earn AS MUCH AS $1.00 CASH
EVERY WEEK!

If You're 12 Years Old or Older, You Can Be a Thoughtful, Discerning LIT Salesman

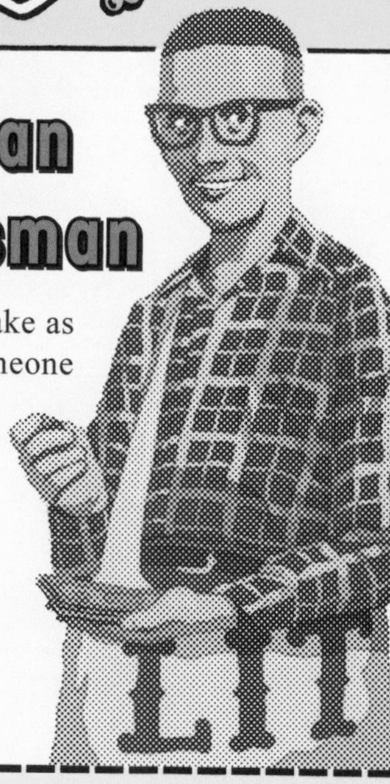
LIT

Join over 100 boys and girls who comprehend metaphors and profundities FREE and make as much as $1.00, selling LIT to friends, neighbors, relatives and others, every week. Someone you know will be eager to buy LIT from you at only $15 a copy, because it contains the full spectrum of human experience, deep meaning, artistic value, and pretty words.

LIT Sells for $15 a Copy . . . You Keep 5¢ Profit!

Yes, 5 ¢ out of every $15 you take in is yours to keep. Sell only 20 copies a week, and you make $1.00 profit each week, and the satisfaction of contributing to the enlightenment of the world… plus valuable knowledge you gain FREE regularly! We'll help you get started now, in a fulfilling business of your own. Mail the Coupon TODAY!

Over 100 Kids Make Money and Grasp Symbolism Without 1¢ Cost

We'll send you LIT right away, by Mail, along with many valuable selling helps. You pay ONLY for the Copies you sell until you know how many to order. Like 100 other kids, 12 or older, you'll find selling LIT is fun – and fulfilling!

MAIL THIS COUPON TODAY!

If coupon is already torn out, print your name, address, age and date of birth and mail it to:

LIT Dept. MC 1 New York, NY
LIT sent to anyone in Continental U.S.

LIT PUBLISHING CO. **PLEASE PRINT**
New York, NY Dept. MC 1
Send my first bundle of LIT, selling helps and symbolism guide.
Name__________
Age_____ Date Born_____ Year_____
In Care of__________
Street__________
Post Office_____ State_____ Zip Code No._____
Print your Favorite Author's Name here

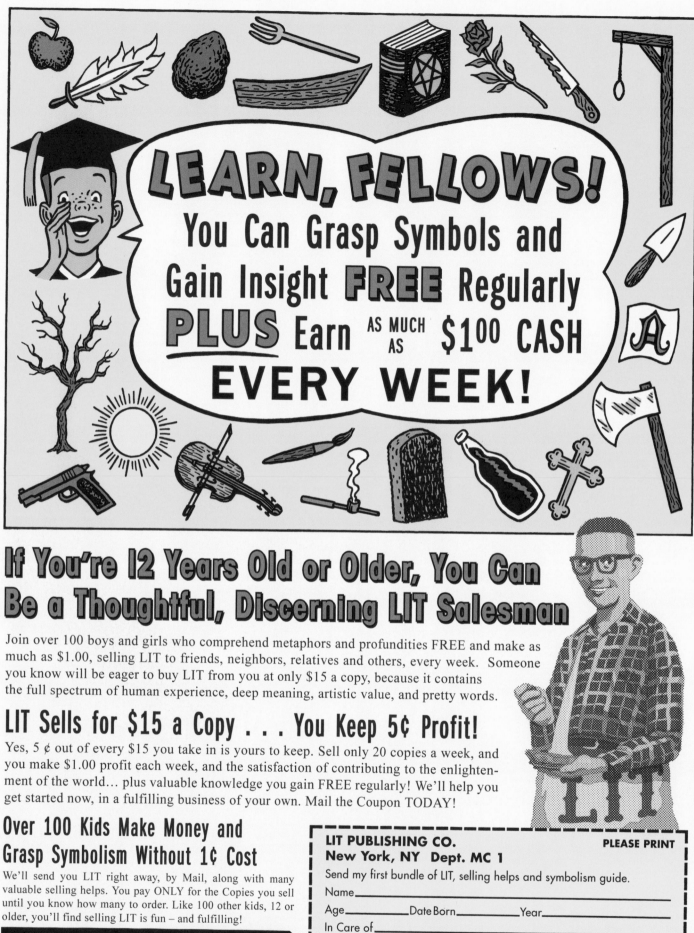

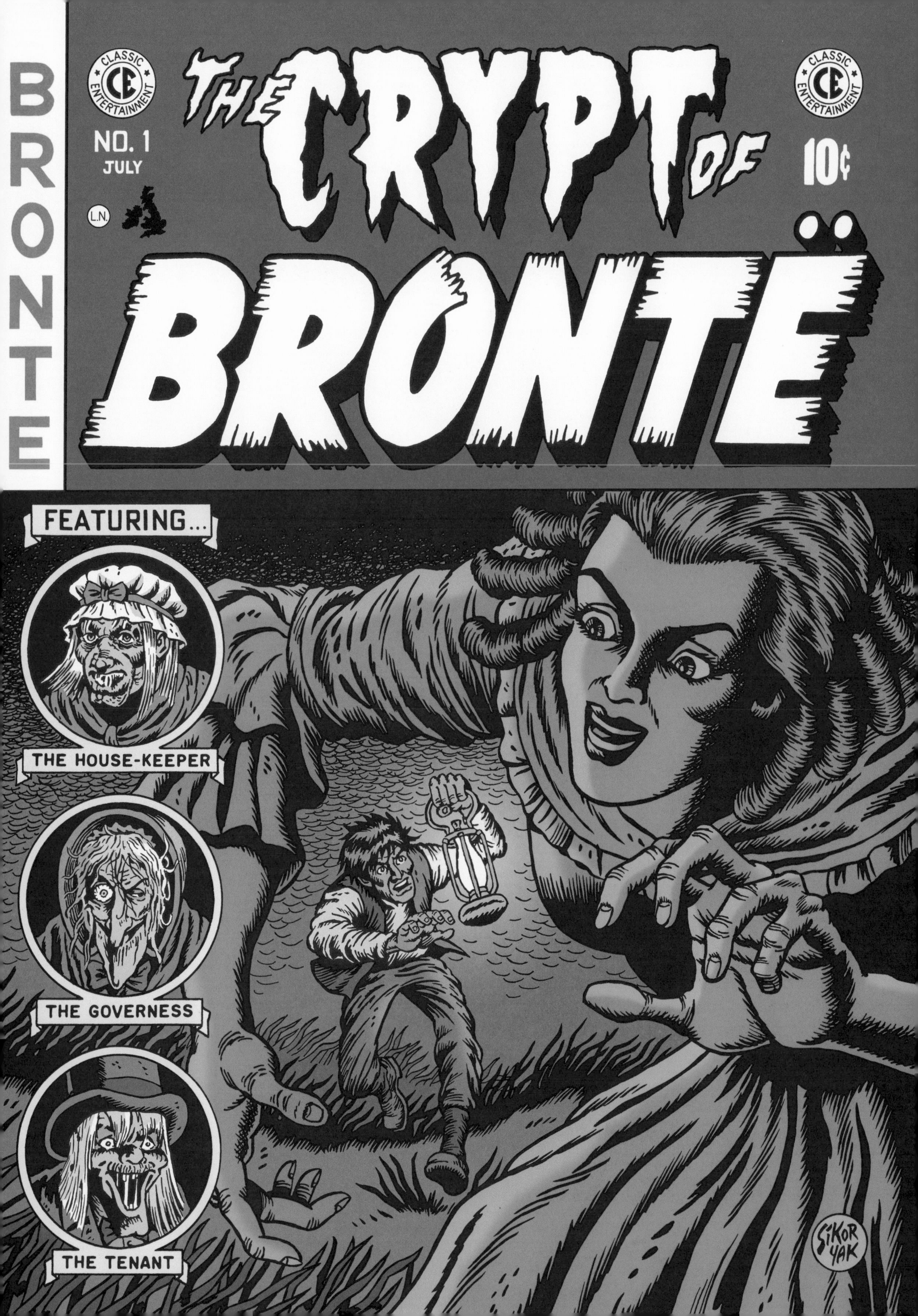
BRONTE
CLASSIC CE ENTERTAINMENT
NO. 1
JULY
L.N.
THE CRYPT OF
BRONTË
CLASSIC CE ENTERTAINMENT
10¢
FEATURING...
THE HOUSE-KEEPER
THE GOVERNESS
THE TENANT
SIKORYAK

THE HOUSE-KEEPER'S TALE

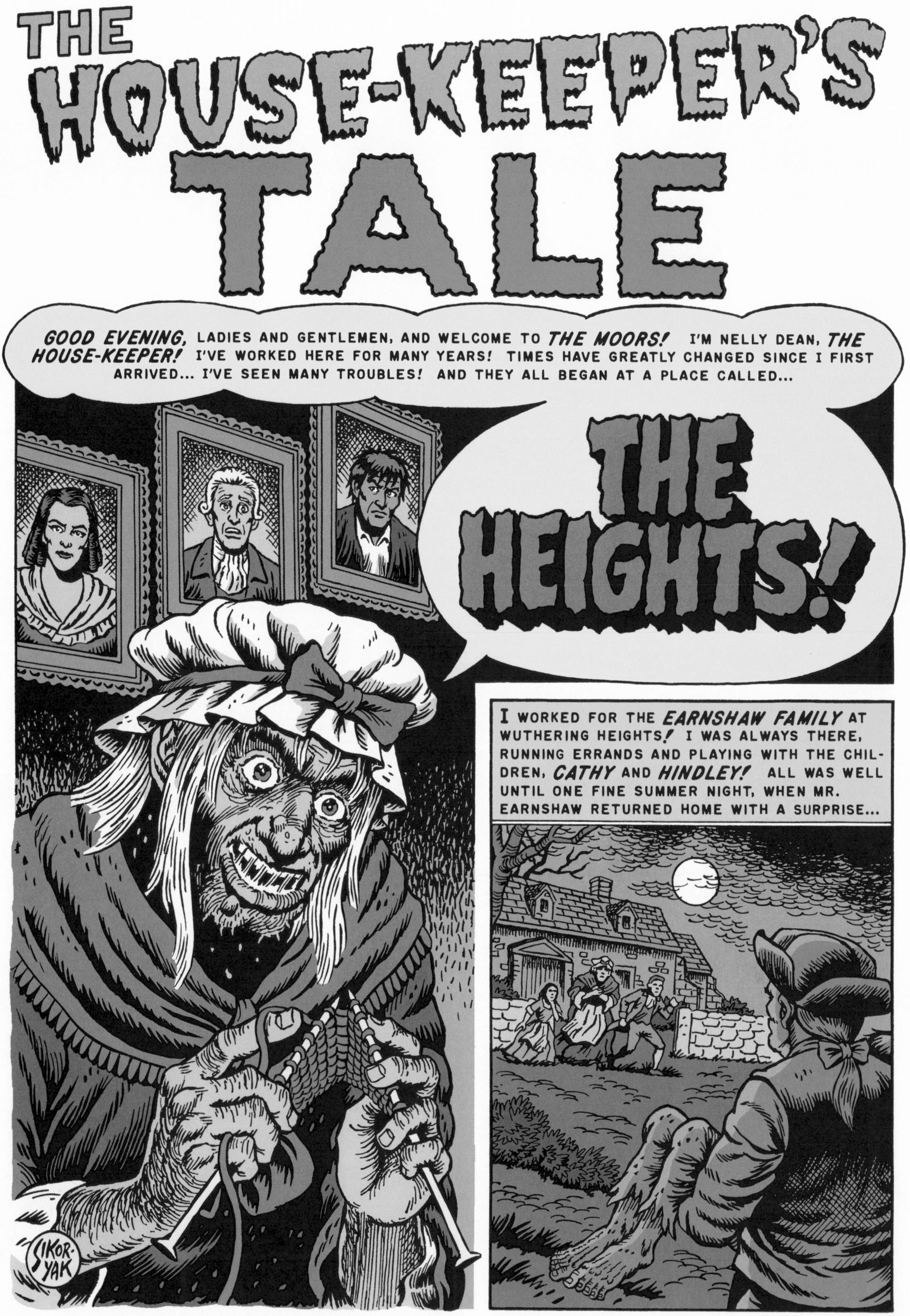
GOOD EVENING, LADIES AND GENTLEMEN, AND WELCOME TO THE MOORS! I'M NELLY DEAN, THE HOUSE-KEEPER! I'VE WORKED HERE FOR MANY YEARS! TIMES HAVE GREATLY CHANGED SINCE I FIRST ARRIVED... I'VE SEEN MANY TROUBLES! AND THEY ALL BEGAN AT A PLACE CALLED...
THE HEIGHTS!
SIKOR-YAK
I WORKED FOR THE EARNSHAW FAMILY AT WUTHERING HEIGHTS! I WAS ALWAYS THERE, RUNNING ERRANDS AND PLAYING WITH THE CHILDREN, CATHY AND HINDLEY! ALL WAS WELL UNTIL ONE FINE SUMMER NIGHT, WHEN MR. EARNSHAW RETURNED HOME WITH A SURPRISE...

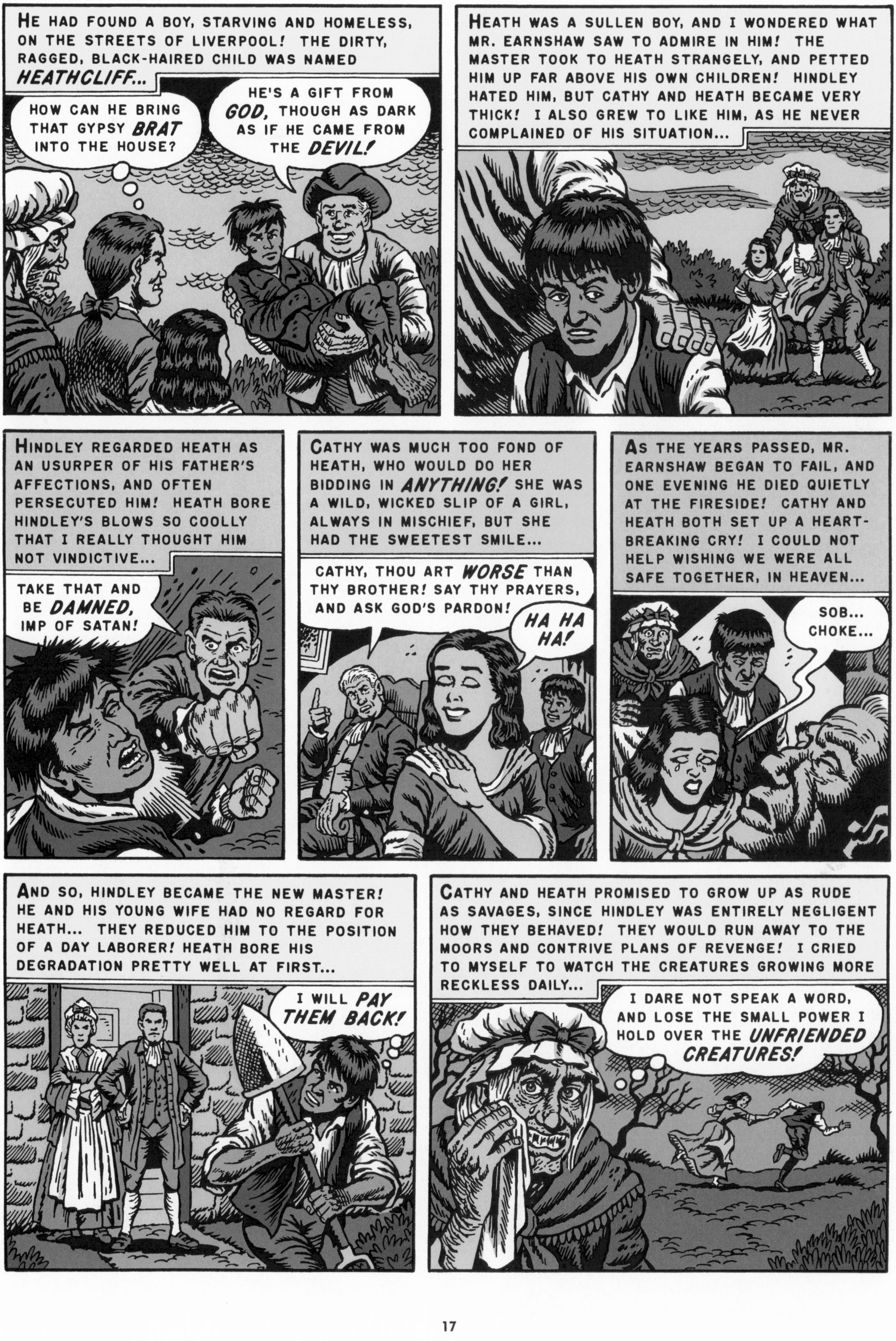
HE HAD FOUND A BOY, STARVING AND HOMELESS, ON THE STREETS OF LIVERPOOL! THE DIRTY, RAGGED, BLACK-HAIRED CHILD WAS NAMED HEATHCLIFF...
HOW CAN HE BRING THAT GYPSY BRAT INTO THE HOUSE?
HE'S A GIFT FROM GOD, THOUGH AS DARK AS IF HE CAME FROM THE DEVIL!
HEATH WAS A SULLEN BOY, AND I WONDERED WHAT MR. EARNSHAW SAW TO ADMIRE IN HIM! THE MASTER TOOK TO HEATH STRANGELY, AND PETTED HIM UP FAR ABOVE HIS OWN CHILDREN! HINDLEY HATED HIM, BUT CATHY AND HEATH BECAME VERY THICK! I ALSO GREW TO LIKE HIM, AS HE NEVER COMPLAINED OF HIS SITUATION...
HINDLEY REGARDED HEATH AS AN USURPER OF HIS FATHER'S AFFECTIONS, AND OFTEN PERSECUTED HIM! HEATH BORE HINDLEY'S BLOWS SO COOLLY THAT I REALLY THOUGHT HIM NOT VINDICTIVE...
TAKE THAT AND BE DAMNED, IMP OF SATAN!
CATHY WAS MUCH TOO FOND OF HEATH, WHO WOULD DO HER BIDDING IN ANYTHING! SHE WAS A WILD, WICKED SLIP OF A GIRL, ALWAYS IN MISCHIEF, BUT SHE HAD THE SWEETEST SMILE...
CATHY, THOU ART WORSE THAN THY BROTHER! SAY THY PRAYERS, AND ASK GOD'S PARDON!
HA HA HA!
AS THE YEARS PASSED, MR. EARNSHAW BEGAN TO FAIL, AND ONE EVENING HE DIED QUIETLY AT THE FIRESIDE! CATHY AND HEATH BOTH SET UP A HEART-BREAKING CRY! I COULD NOT HELP WISHING WE WERE ALL SAFE TOGETHER, IN HEAVEN...
SOB... CHOKE...
AND SO, HINDLEY BECAME THE NEW MASTER! HE AND HIS YOUNG WIFE HAD NO REGARD FOR HEATH... THEY REDUCED HIM TO THE POSITION OF A DAY LABORER! HEATH BORE HIS DEGRADATION PRETTY WELL AT FIRST...
I WILL PAY THEM BACK!
CATHY AND HEATH PROMISED TO GROW UP AS RUDE AS SAVAGES, SINCE HINDLEY WAS ENTIRELY NEGLIGENT HOW THEY BEHAVED! THEY WOULD RUN AWAY TO THE MOORS AND CONTRIVE PLANS OF REVENGE! I CRIED TO MYSELF TO WATCH THE CREATURES GROWING MORE RECKLESS DAILY...
I DARE NOT SPEAK A WORD, AND LOSE THE SMALL POWER I HOLD OVER THE UNFRIENDED CREATURES!

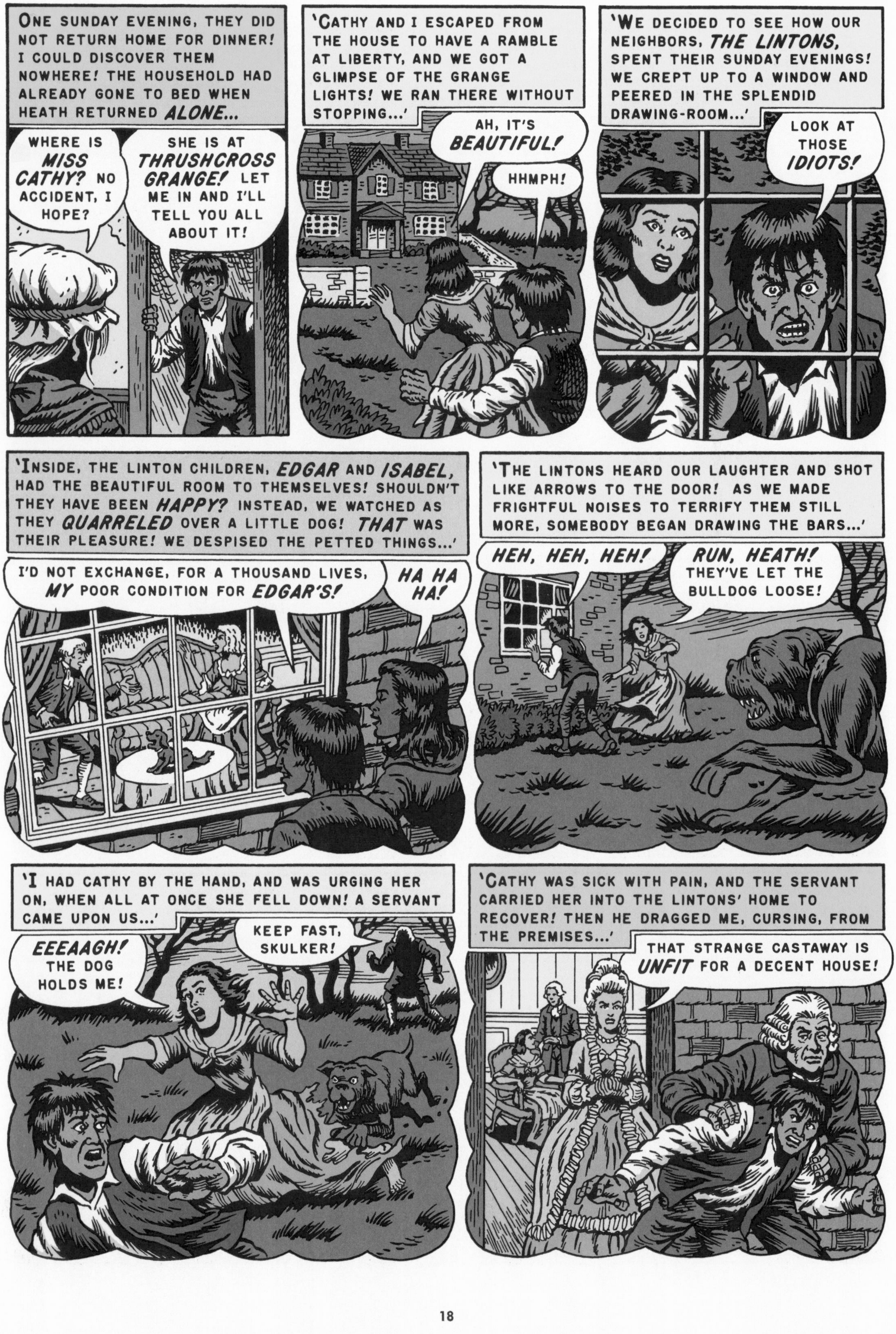
One Sunday evening, they did not return home for dinner! I could discover them nowhere! The household had already gone to bed when Heath returned *alone*...
Where is *Miss Cathy?* No accident, I hope?
She is at *Thrushcross Grange!* Let me in and I'll tell you all about it!
'Cathy and I escaped from the house to have a ramble at liberty, and we got a glimpse of the Grange lights! We ran there without stopping...'
Ah, it's *beautiful!*
Hhmph!
'We decided to see how our neighbors, *The Lintons,* spent their Sunday evenings! We crept up to a window and peered in the splendid drawing-room...'
Look at those *idiots!*
'Inside, the Linton children, *Edgar* and *Isabel,* had the beautiful room to themselves! Shouldn't they have been *happy?* Instead, we watched as they *quarreled* over a little dog! *That* was their pleasure! We despised the petted things...'
I'd not exchange, for a thousand lives, *my* poor condition for *Edgar's!*
Ha ha ha!
'The Lintons heard our laughter and shot like arrows to the door! As we made frightful noises to terrify them still more, somebody began drawing the bars...'
Heh, heh, heh!
Run, Heath! They've let the bulldog loose!
'I had Cathy by the hand, and was urging her on, when all at once she fell down! A servant came upon us...'
Eeeaagh! The dog holds me!
Keep fast, Skulker!
'Cathy was sick with pain, and the servant carried her into the Lintons' home to recover! Then he dragged me, cursing, from the premises...'
That strange castaway is *unfit* for a decent house!

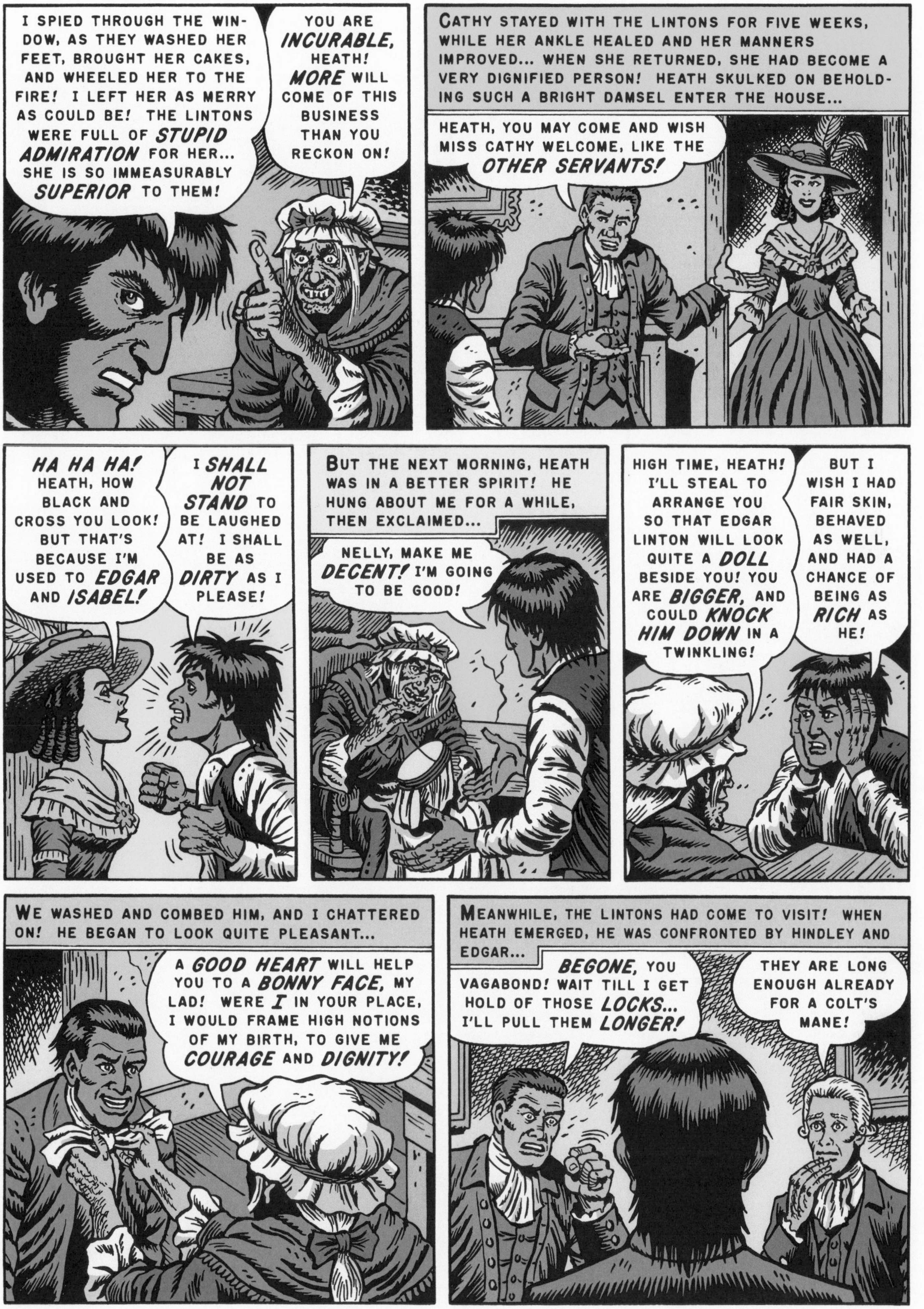
I SPIED THROUGH THE WINDOW, AS THEY WASHED HER FEET, BROUGHT HER CAKES, AND WHEELED HER TO THE FIRE! I LEFT HER AS MERRY AS COULD BE! THE LINTONS WERE FULL OF STUPID ADMIRATION FOR HER... SHE IS SO IMMEASURABLY SUPERIOR TO THEM!
YOU ARE INCURABLE, HEATH! MORE WILL COME OF THIS BUSINESS THAN YOU RECKON ON!
CATHY STAYED WITH THE LINTONS FOR FIVE WEEKS, WHILE HER ANKLE HEALED AND HER MANNERS IMPROVED... WHEN SHE RETURNED, SHE HAD BECOME A VERY DIGNIFIED PERSON! HEATH SKULKED ON BEHOLDING SUCH A BRIGHT DAMSEL ENTER THE HOUSE...
HEATH, YOU MAY COME AND WISH MISS CATHY WELCOME, LIKE THE OTHER SERVANTS!
HA HA HA! HEATH, HOW BLACK AND CROSS YOU LOOK! BUT THAT'S BECAUSE I'M USED TO EDGAR AND ISABEL!
I SHALL NOT STAND TO BE LAUGHED AT! I SHALL BE AS DIRTY AS I PLEASE!
BUT THE NEXT MORNING, HEATH WAS IN A BETTER SPIRIT! HE HUNG ABOUT ME FOR A WHILE, THEN EXCLAIMED...
NELLY, MAKE ME DECENT! I'M GOING TO BE GOOD!
HIGH TIME, HEATH! I'LL STEAL TO ARRANGE YOU SO THAT EDGAR LINTON WILL LOOK QUITE A DOLL BESIDE YOU! YOU ARE BIGGER, AND COULD KNOCK HIM DOWN IN A TWINKLING!
BUT I WISH I HAD FAIR SKIN, BEHAVED AS WELL, AND HAD A CHANCE OF BEING AS RICH AS HE!
WE WASHED AND COMBED HIM, AND I CHATTERED ON! HE BEGAN TO LOOK QUITE PLEASANT...
A GOOD HEART WILL HELP YOU TO A BONNY FACE, MY LAD! WERE I IN YOUR PLACE, I WOULD FRAME HIGH NOTIONS OF MY BIRTH, TO GIVE ME COURAGE AND DIGNITY!
MEANWHILE, THE LINTONS HAD COME TO VISIT! WHEN HEATH EMERGED, HE WAS CONFRONTED BY HINDLEY AND EDGAR...
BEGONE, YOU VAGABOND! WAIT TILL I GET HOLD OF THOSE LOCKS... I'LL PULL THEM LONGER!
THEY ARE LONG ENOUGH ALREADY FOR A COLT'S MANE!

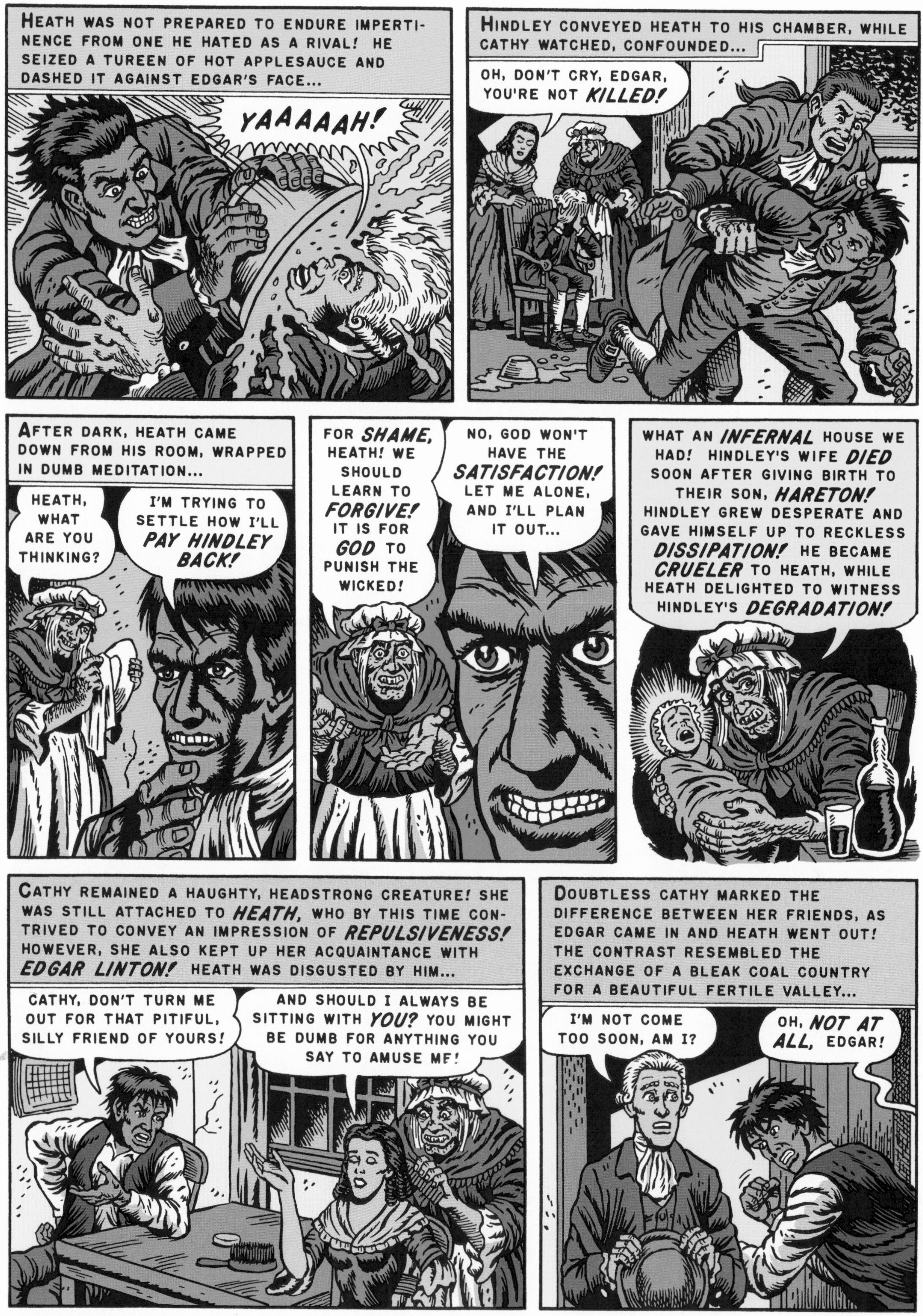
HEATH WAS NOT PREPARED TO ENDURE IMPERTINENCE FROM ONE HE HATED AS A RIVAL! HE SEIZED A TUREEN OF HOT APPLESAUCE AND DASHED IT AGAINST EDGAR'S FACE...
YAAAAAH!
HINDLEY CONVEYED HEATH TO HIS CHAMBER, WHILE CATHY WATCHED, CONFOUNDED...
OH, DON'T CRY, EDGAR, YOU'RE NOT KILLED!
AFTER DARK, HEATH CAME DOWN FROM HIS ROOM, WRAPPED IN DUMB MEDITATION...
HEATH, WHAT ARE YOU THINKING?
I'M TRYING TO SETTLE HOW I'LL PAY HINDLEY BACK!
FOR SHAME, HEATH! WE SHOULD LEARN TO FORGIVE! IT IS FOR GOD TO PUNISH THE WICKED!
NO, GOD WON'T HAVE THE SATISFACTION! LET ME ALONE, AND I'LL PLAN IT OUT...
WHAT AN INFERNAL HOUSE WE HAD! HINDLEY'S WIFE DIED SOON AFTER GIVING BIRTH TO THEIR SON, HARETON! HINDLEY GREW DESPERATE AND GAVE HIMSELF UP TO RECKLESS DISSIPATION! HE BECAME CRUELER TO HEATH, WHILE HEATH DELIGHTED TO WITNESS HINDLEY'S DEGRADATION!
CATHY REMAINED A HAUGHTY, HEADSTRONG CREATURE! SHE WAS STILL ATTACHED TO HEATH, WHO BY THIS TIME CONTRIVED TO CONVEY AN IMPRESSION OF REPULSIVENESS! HOWEVER, SHE ALSO KEPT UP HER ACQUAINTANCE WITH EDGAR LINTON! HEATH WAS DISGUSTED BY HIM...
CATHY, DON'T TURN ME OUT FOR THAT PITIFUL, SILLY FRIEND OF YOURS!
AND SHOULD I ALWAYS BE SITTING WITH YOU? YOU MIGHT BE DUMB FOR ANYTHING YOU SAY TO AMUSE ME!
DOUBTLESS CATHY MARKED THE DIFFERENCE BETWEEN HER FRIENDS, AS EDGAR CAME IN AND HEATH WENT OUT! THE CONTRAST RESEMBLED THE EXCHANGE OF A BLEAK COAL COUNTRY FOR A BEAUTIFUL FERTILE VALLEY...
I'M NOT COME TOO SOON, AM I?
OH, NOT AT ALL, EDGAR!

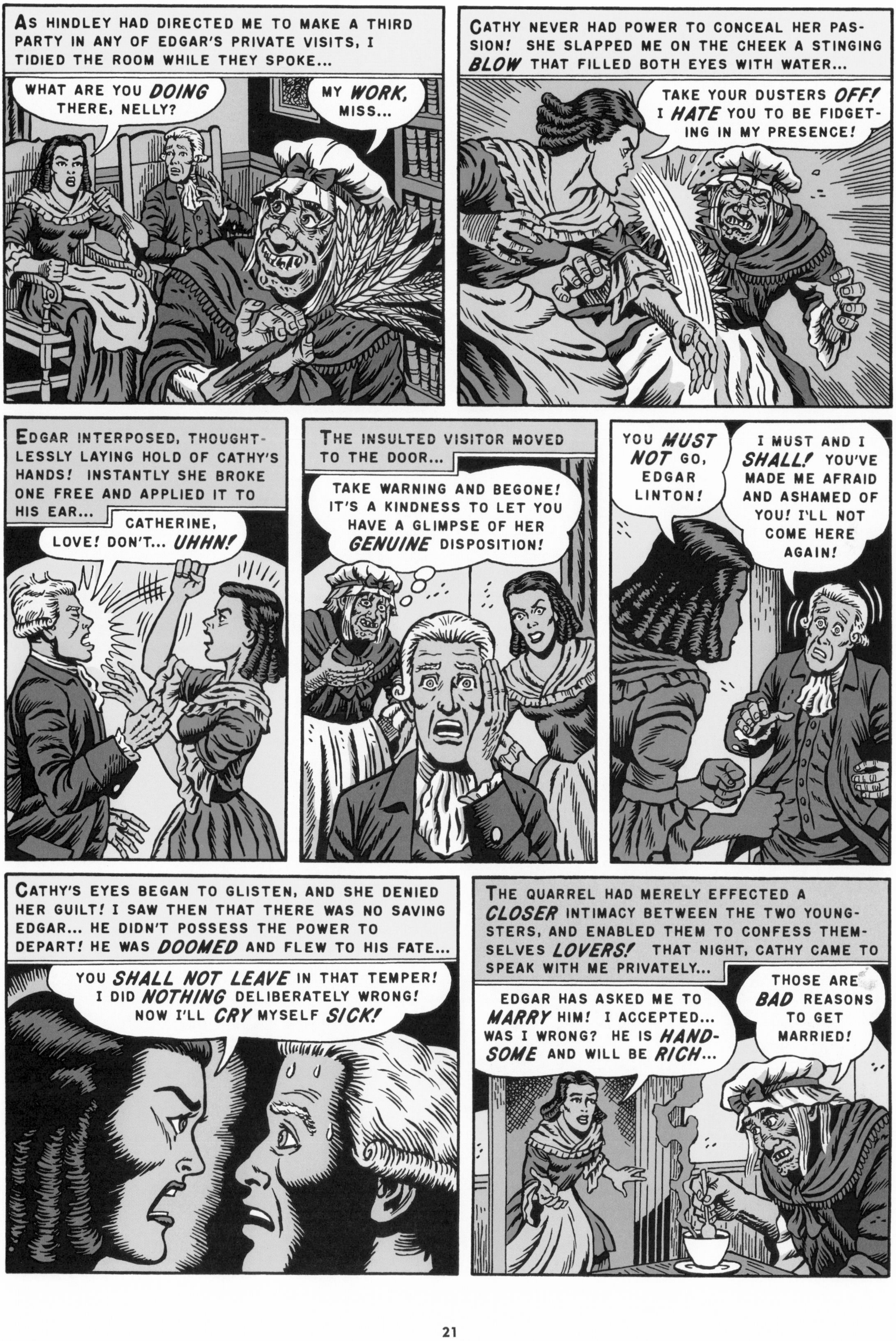
AS HINDLEY HAD DIRECTED ME TO MAKE A THIRD PARTY IN ANY OF EDGAR'S PRIVATE VISITS, I TIDIED THE ROOM WHILE THEY SPOKE...
WHAT ARE YOU DOING THERE, NELLY?
MY WORK, MISS...
CATHY NEVER HAD POWER TO CONCEAL HER PASSION! SHE SLAPPED ME ON THE CHEEK A STINGING BLOW THAT FILLED BOTH EYES WITH WATER...
TAKE YOUR DUSTERS OFF! I HATE YOU TO BE FIDGETING IN MY PRESENCE!
EDGAR INTERPOSED, THOUGHTLESSLY LAYING HOLD OF CATHY'S HANDS! INSTANTLY SHE BROKE ONE FREE AND APPLIED IT TO HIS EAR...
CATHERINE, LOVE! DON'T... UHHN!
THE INSULTED VISITOR MOVED TO THE DOOR...
TAKE WARNING AND BEGONE! IT'S A KINDNESS TO LET YOU HAVE A GLIMPSE OF HER GENUINE DISPOSITION!
YOU MUST NOT GO, EDGAR LINTON!
I MUST AND I SHALL! YOU'VE MADE ME AFRAID AND ASHAMED OF YOU! I'LL NOT COME HERE AGAIN!
CATHY'S EYES BEGAN TO GLISTEN, AND SHE DENIED HER GUILT! I SAW THEN THAT THERE WAS NO SAVING EDGAR... HE DIDN'T POSSESS THE POWER TO DEPART! HE WAS DOOMED AND FLEW TO HIS FATE...
YOU SHALL NOT LEAVE IN THAT TEMPER! I DID NOTHING DELIBERATELY WRONG! NOW I'LL CRY MYSELF SICK!
THE QUARREL HAD MERELY EFFECTED A CLOSER INTIMACY BETWEEN THE TWO YOUNGSTERS, AND ENABLED THEM TO CONFESS THEMSELVES LOVERS! THAT NIGHT, CATHY CAME TO SPEAK WITH ME PRIVATELY...
EDGAR HAS ASKED ME TO MARRY HIM! I ACCEPTED... WAS I WRONG? HE IS HANDSOME AND WILL BE RICH...
THOSE ARE BAD REASONS TO GET MARRIED!

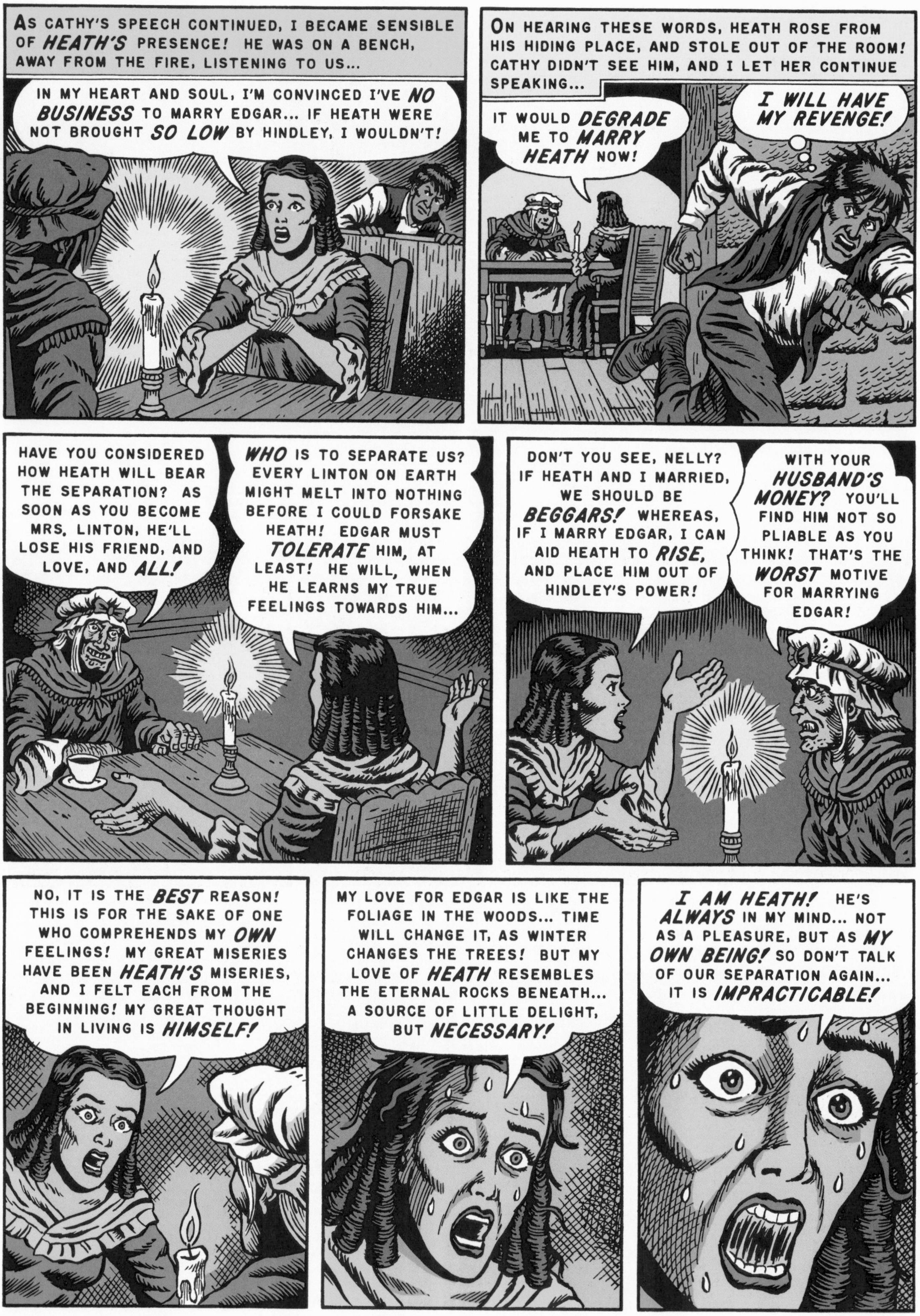

AS CATHY'S SPEECH CONTINUED, I BECAME SENSIBLE OF HEATH'S PRESENCE! HE WAS ON A BENCH, AWAY FROM THE FIRE, LISTENING TO US...
IN MY HEART AND SOUL, I'M CONVINCED I'VE NO BUSINESS TO MARRY EDGAR... IF HEATH WERE NOT BROUGHT SO LOW BY HINDLEY, I WOULDN'T!
ON HEARING THESE WORDS, HEATH ROSE FROM HIS HIDING PLACE, AND STOLE OUT OF THE ROOM! CATHY DIDN'T SEE HIM, AND I LET HER CONTINUE SPEAKING...
IT WOULD DEGRADE ME TO MARRY HEATH NOW!
I WILL HAVE MY REVENGE!
HAVE YOU CONSIDERED HOW HEATH WILL BEAR THE SEPARATION? AS SOON AS YOU BECOME MRS. LINTON, HE'LL LOSE HIS FRIEND, AND LOVE, AND ALL!
WHO IS TO SEPARATE US? EVERY LINTON ON EARTH MIGHT MELT INTO NOTHING BEFORE I COULD FORSAKE HEATH! EDGAR MUST TOLERATE HIM, AT LEAST! HE WILL, WHEN HE LEARNS MY TRUE FEELINGS TOWARDS HIM...
DON'T YOU SEE, NELLY? IF HEATH AND I MARRIED, WE SHOULD BE BEGGARS! WHEREAS, IF I MARRY EDGAR, I CAN AID HEATH TO RISE, AND PLACE HIM OUT OF HINDLEY'S POWER!
WITH YOUR HUSBAND'S MONEY? YOU'LL FIND HIM NOT SO PLIABLE AS YOU THINK! THAT'S THE WORST MOTIVE FOR MARRYING EDGAR!
NO, IT IS THE BEST REASON! THIS IS FOR THE SAKE OF ONE WHO COMPREHENDS MY OWN FEELINGS! MY GREAT MISERIES HAVE BEEN HEATH'S MISERIES, AND I FELT EACH FROM THE BEGINNING! MY GREAT THOUGHT IN LIVING IS HIMSELF!
MY LOVE FOR EDGAR IS LIKE THE FOLIAGE IN THE WOODS... TIME WILL CHANGE IT, AS WINTER CHANGES THE TREES! BUT MY LOVE OF HEATH RESEMBLES THE ETERNAL ROCKS BENEATH... A SOURCE OF LITTLE DELIGHT, BUT NECESSARY!
I AM HEATH! HE'S ALWAYS IN MY MIND... NOT AS A PLEASURE, BUT AS MY OWN BEING! SO DON'T TALK OF OUR SEPARATION AGAIN... IT IS IMPRACTICABLE!

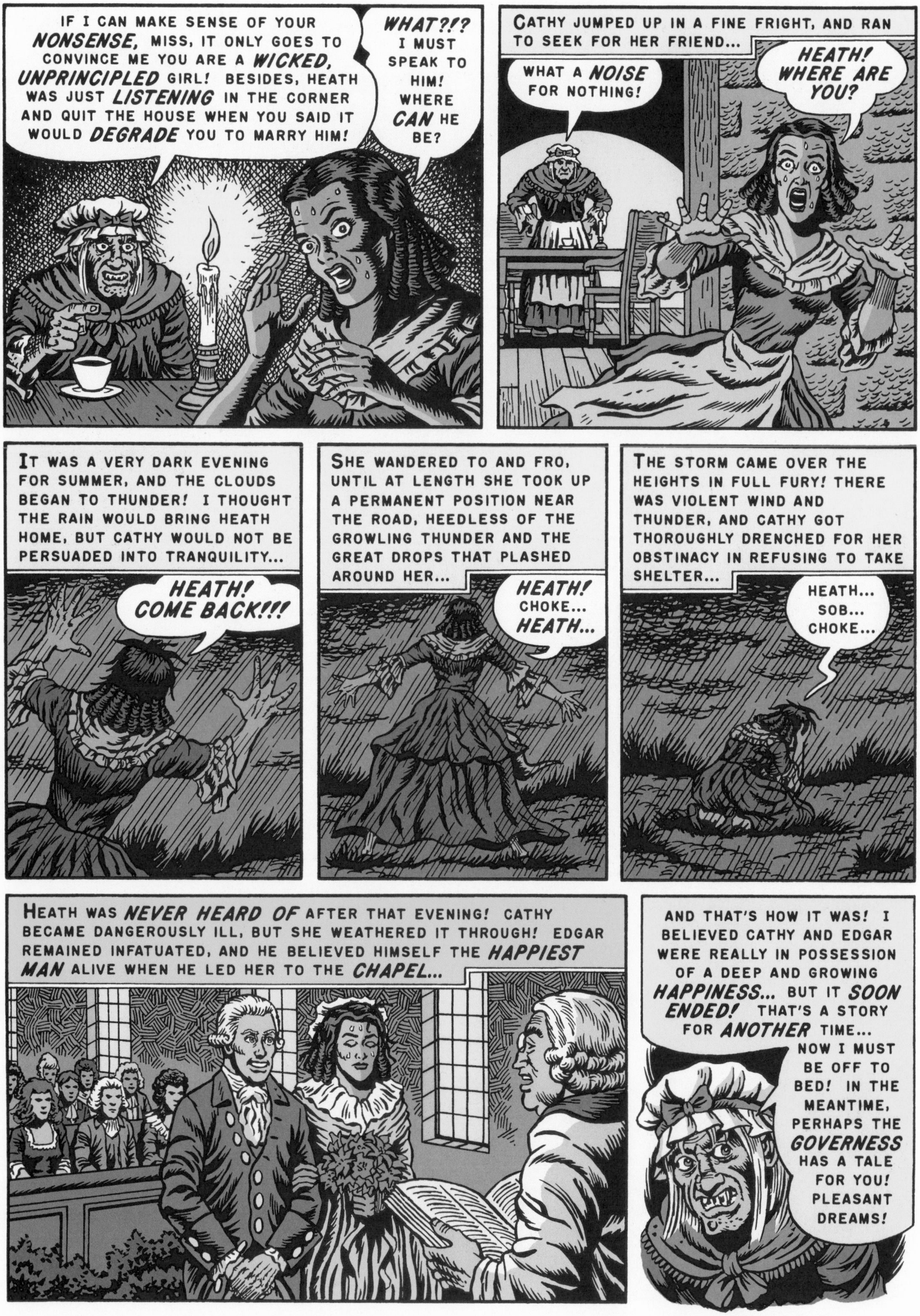

IF I CAN MAKE SENSE OF YOUR NONSENSE, MISS, IT ONLY GOES TO CONVINCE ME YOU ARE A WICKED, UNPRINCIPLED GIRL! BESIDES, HEATH WAS JUST LISTENING IN THE CORNER AND QUIT THE HOUSE WHEN YOU SAID IT WOULD DEGRADE YOU TO MARRY HIM!
WHAT?!? I MUST SPEAK TO HIM! WHERE CAN HE BE?
CATHY JUMPED UP IN A FINE FRIGHT, AND RAN TO SEEK FOR HER FRIEND...
WHAT A NOISE FOR NOTHING!
HEATH! WHERE ARE YOU?
IT WAS A VERY DARK EVENING FOR SUMMER, AND THE CLOUDS BEGAN TO THUNDER! I THOUGHT THE RAIN WOULD BRING HEATH HOME, BUT CATHY WOULD NOT BE PERSUADED INTO TRANQUILITY...
HEATH! COME BACK!!!
SHE WANDERED TO AND FRO, UNTIL AT LENGTH SHE TOOK UP A PERMANENT POSITION NEAR THE ROAD, HEEDLESS OF THE GROWLING THUNDER AND THE GREAT DROPS THAT PLASHED AROUND HER...
HEATH! CHOKE... HEATH...
THE STORM CAME OVER THE HEIGHTS IN FULL FURY! THERE WAS VIOLENT WIND AND THUNDER, AND CATHY GOT THOROUGHLY DRENCHED FOR HER OBSTINACY IN REFUSING TO TAKE SHELTER...
HEATH... SOB... CHOKE...
HEATH WAS NEVER HEARD OF AFTER THAT EVENING! CATHY BECAME DANGEROUSLY ILL, BUT SHE WEATHERED IT THROUGH! EDGAR REMAINED INFATUATED, AND HE BELIEVED HIMSELF THE HAPPIEST MAN ALIVE WHEN HE LED HER TO THE CHAPEL...
AND THAT'S HOW IT WAS! I BELIEVED CATHY AND EDGAR WERE REALLY IN POSSESSION OF A DEEP AND GROWING HAPPINESS... BUT IT SOON ENDED! THAT'S A STORY FOR ANOTHER TIME... NOW I MUST BE OFF TO BED! IN THE MEANTIME, PERHAPS THE GOVERNESS HAS A TALE FOR YOU! PLEASANT DREAMS!

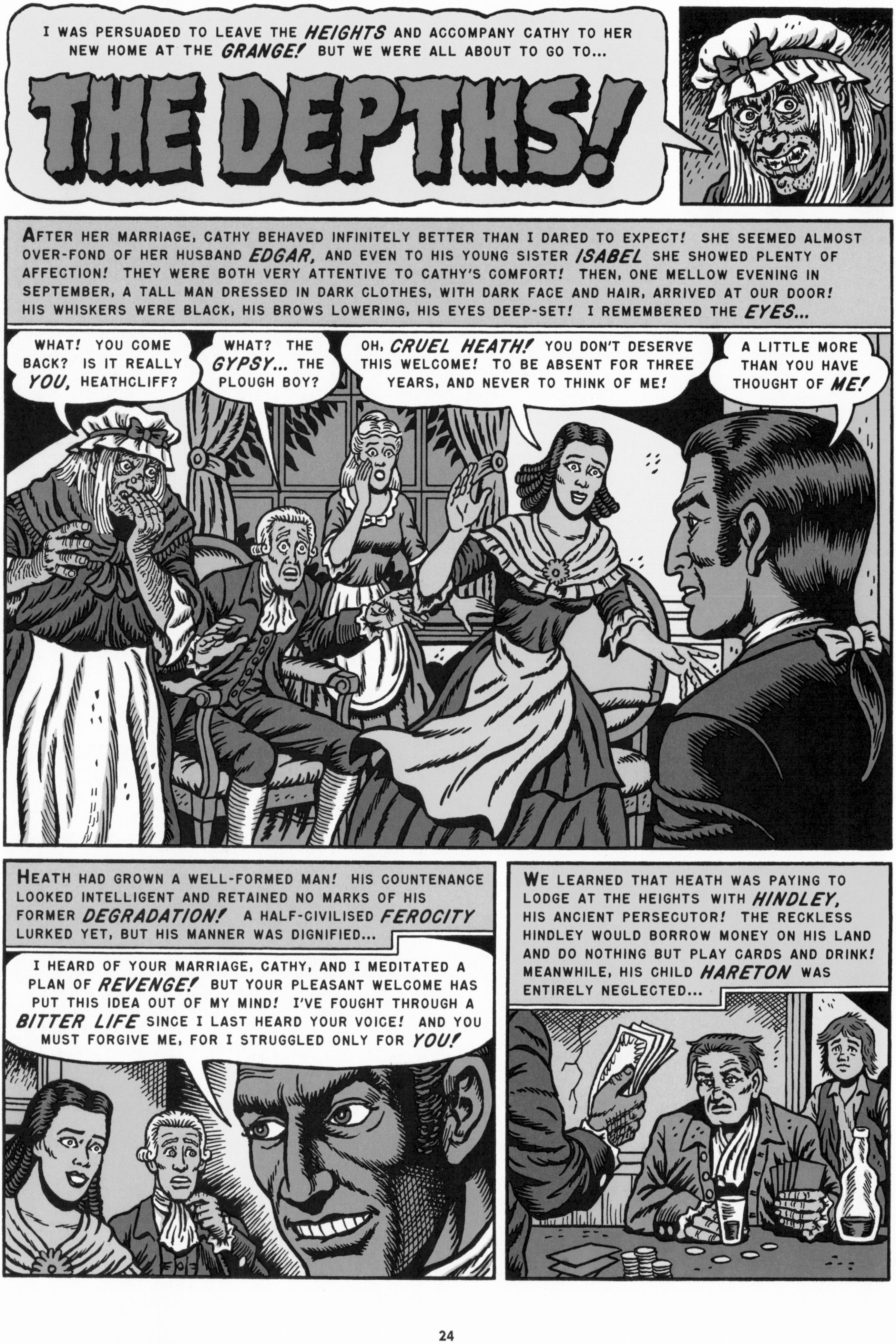
I WAS PERSUADED TO LEAVE THE HEIGHTS AND ACCOMPANY CATHY TO HER NEW HOME AT THE GRANGE! BUT WE WERE ALL ABOUT TO GO TO...
THE DEPTHS!
AFTER HER MARRIAGE, CATHY BEHAVED INFINITELY BETTER THAN I DARED TO EXPECT! SHE SEEMED ALMOST OVER-FOND OF HER HUSBAND EDGAR, AND EVEN TO HIS YOUNG SISTER ISABEL SHE SHOWED PLENTY OF AFFECTION! THEY WERE BOTH VERY ATTENTIVE TO CATHY'S COMFORT! THEN, ONE MELLOW EVENING IN SEPTEMBER, A TALL MAN DRESSED IN DARK CLOTHES, WITH DARK FACE AND HAIR, ARRIVED AT OUR DOOR! HIS WHISKERS WERE BLACK, HIS BROWS LOWERING, HIS EYES DEEP-SET! I REMEMBERED THE EYES...
WHAT! YOU COME BACK? IS IT REALLY YOU, HEATHCLIFF?
WHAT? THE GYPSY... THE PLOUGH BOY?
OH, CRUEL HEATH! YOU DON'T DESERVE THIS WELCOME! TO BE ABSENT FOR THREE YEARS, AND NEVER TO THINK OF ME!
A LITTLE MORE THAN YOU HAVE THOUGHT OF ME!
HEATH HAD GROWN A WELL-FORMED MAN! HIS COUNTENANCE LOOKED INTELLIGENT AND RETAINED NO MARKS OF HIS FORMER DEGRADATION! A HALF-CIVILISED FEROCITY LURKED YET, BUT HIS MANNER WAS DIGNIFIED...
I HEARD OF YOUR MARRIAGE, CATHY, AND I MEDITATED A PLAN OF REVENGE! BUT YOUR PLEASANT WELCOME HAS PUT THIS IDEA OUT OF MY MIND! I'VE FOUGHT THROUGH A BITTER LIFE SINCE I LAST HEARD YOUR VOICE! AND YOU MUST FORGIVE ME, FOR I STRUGGLED ONLY FOR YOU!
WE LEARNED THAT HEATH WAS PAYING TO LODGE AT THE HEIGHTS WITH HINDLEY, HIS ANCIENT PERSECUTOR! THE RECKLESS HINDLEY WOULD BORROW MONEY ON HIS LAND AND DO NOTHING BUT PLAY CARDS AND DRINK! MEANWHILE, HIS CHILD HARETON WAS ENTIRELY NEGLECTED...

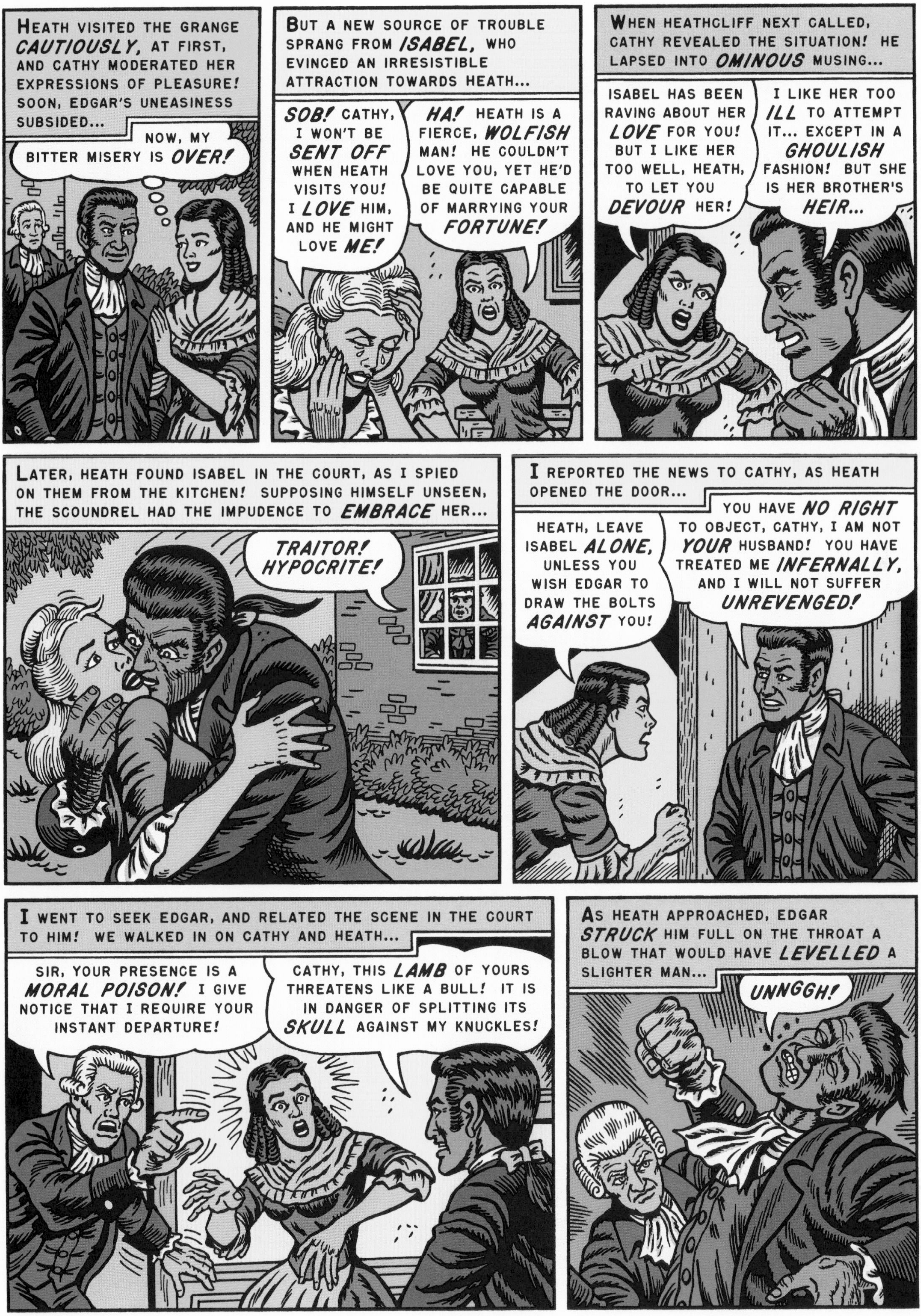
HEATH VISITED THE GRANGE CAUTIOUSLY, AT FIRST, AND CATHY MODERATED HER EXPRESSIONS OF PLEASURE! SOON, EDGAR'S UNEASINESS SUBSIDED...
NOW, MY BITTER MISERY IS OVER!
BUT A NEW SOURCE OF TROUBLE SPRANG FROM ISABEL, WHO EVINCED AN IRRESISTIBLE ATTRACTION TOWARDS HEATH...
SOB! CATHY, I WON'T BE SENT OFF WHEN HEATH VISITS YOU! I LOVE HIM, AND HE MIGHT LOVE ME!
HA! HEATH IS A FIERCE, WOLFISH MAN! HE COULDN'T LOVE YOU, YET HE'D BE QUITE CAPABLE OF MARRYING YOUR FORTUNE!
WHEN HEATHCLIFF NEXT CALLED, CATHY REVEALED THE SITUATION! HE LAPSED INTO OMINOUS MUSING...
ISABEL HAS BEEN RAVING ABOUT HER LOVE FOR YOU! BUT I LIKE HER TOO WELL, HEATH, TO LET YOU DEVOUR HER!
I LIKE HER TOO ILL TO ATTEMPT IT... EXCEPT IN A GHOULISH FASHION! BUT SHE IS HER BROTHER'S HEIR...
LATER, HEATH FOUND ISABEL IN THE COURT, AS I SPIED ON THEM FROM THE KITCHEN! SUPPOSING HIMSELF UNSEEN, THE SCOUNDREL HAD THE IMPUDENCE TO EMBRACE HER...
TRAITOR! HYPOCRITE!
I REPORTED THE NEWS TO CATHY, AS HEATH OPENED THE DOOR...
HEATH, LEAVE ISABEL ALONE, UNLESS YOU WISH EDGAR TO DRAW THE BOLTS AGAINST YOU!
YOU HAVE NO RIGHT TO OBJECT, CATHY, I AM NOT YOUR HUSBAND! YOU HAVE TREATED ME INFERNALLY, AND I WILL NOT SUFFER UNREVENGED!
I WENT TO SEEK EDGAR, AND RELATED THE SCENE IN THE COURT TO HIM! WE WALKED IN ON CATHY AND HEATH...
SIR, YOUR PRESENCE IS A MORAL POISON! I GIVE NOTICE THAT I REQUIRE YOUR INSTANT DEPARTURE!
CATHY, THIS LAMB OF YOURS THREATENS LIKE A BULL! IT IS IN DANGER OF SPLITTING ITS SKULL AGAINST MY KNUCKLES!
AS HEATH APPROACHED, EDGAR STRUCK HIM FULL ON THE THROAT A BLOW THAT WOULD HAVE LEVELLED A SLIGHTER MAN...
UNNGGH!

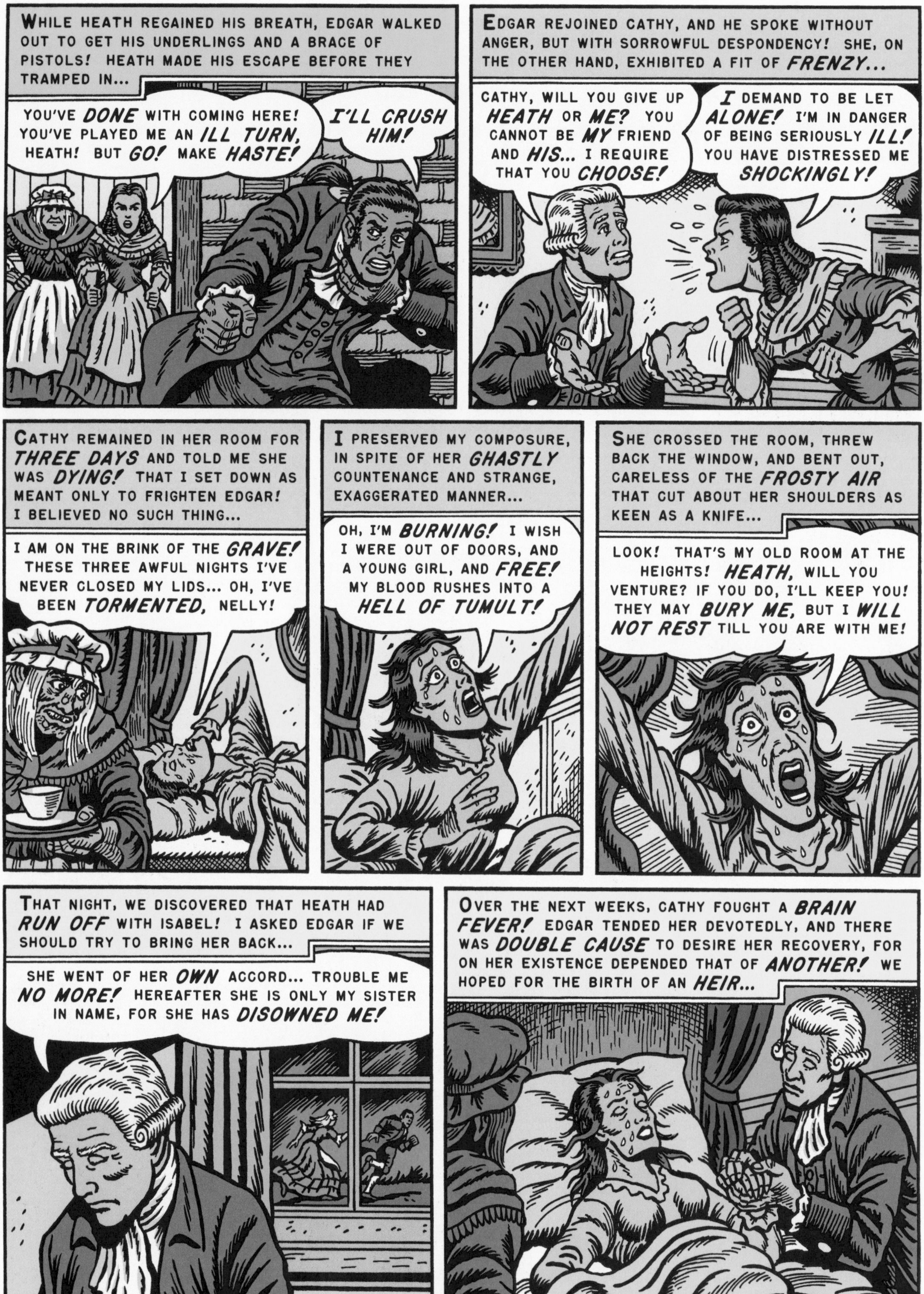
WHILE HEATH REGAINED HIS BREATH, EDGAR WALKED OUT TO GET HIS UNDERLINGS AND A BRACE OF PISTOLS! HEATH MADE HIS ESCAPE BEFORE THEY TRAMPED IN...
YOU'VE DONE WITH COMING HERE! YOU'VE PLAYED ME AN ILL TURN, HEATH! BUT GO! MAKE HASTE!
I'LL CRUSH HIM!
EDGAR REJOINED CATHY, AND HE SPOKE WITHOUT ANGER, BUT WITH SORROWFUL DESPONDENCY! SHE, ON THE OTHER HAND, EXHIBITED A FIT OF FRENZY...
CATHY, WILL YOU GIVE UP HEATH OR ME? YOU CANNOT BE MY FRIEND AND HIS... I REQUIRE THAT YOU CHOOSE!
I DEMAND TO BE LET ALONE! I'M IN DANGER OF BEING SERIOUSLY ILL! YOU HAVE DISTRESSED ME SHOCKINGLY!
CATHY REMAINED IN HER ROOM FOR THREE DAYS AND TOLD ME SHE WAS DYING! THAT I SET DOWN AS MEANT ONLY TO FRIGHTEN EDGAR! I BELIEVED NO SUCH THING...
I AM ON THE BRINK OF THE GRAVE! THESE THREE AWFUL NIGHTS I'VE NEVER CLOSED MY LIDS... OH, I'VE BEEN TORMENTED, NELLY!
I PRESERVED MY COMPOSURE, IN SPITE OF HER GHASTLY COUNTENANCE AND STRANGE, EXAGGERATED MANNER...
OH, I'M BURNING! I WISH I WERE OUT OF DOORS, AND A YOUNG GIRL, AND FREE! MY BLOOD RUSHES INTO A HELL OF TUMULT!
SHE CROSSED THE ROOM, THREW BACK THE WINDOW, AND BENT OUT, CARELESS OF THE FROSTY AIR THAT CUT ABOUT HER SHOULDERS AS KEEN AS A KNIFE...
LOOK! THAT'S MY OLD ROOM AT THE HEIGHTS! HEATH, WILL YOU VENTURE? IF YOU DO, I'LL KEEP YOU! THEY MAY BURY ME, BUT I WILL NOT REST TILL YOU ARE WITH ME!
THAT NIGHT, WE DISCOVERED THAT HEATH HAD RUN OFF WITH ISABEL! I ASKED EDGAR IF WE SHOULD TRY TO BRING HER BACK...
SHE WENT OF HER OWN ACCORD... TROUBLE ME NO MORE! HEREAFTER SHE IS ONLY MY SISTER IN NAME, FOR SHE HAS DISOWNED ME!
OVER THE NEXT WEEKS, CATHY FOUGHT A BRAIN FEVER! EDGAR TENDED HER DEVOTEDLY, AND THERE WAS DOUBLE CAUSE TO DESIRE HER RECOVERY, FOR ON HER EXISTENCE DEPENDED THAT OF ANOTHER! WE HOPED FOR THE BIRTH OF AN HEIR...

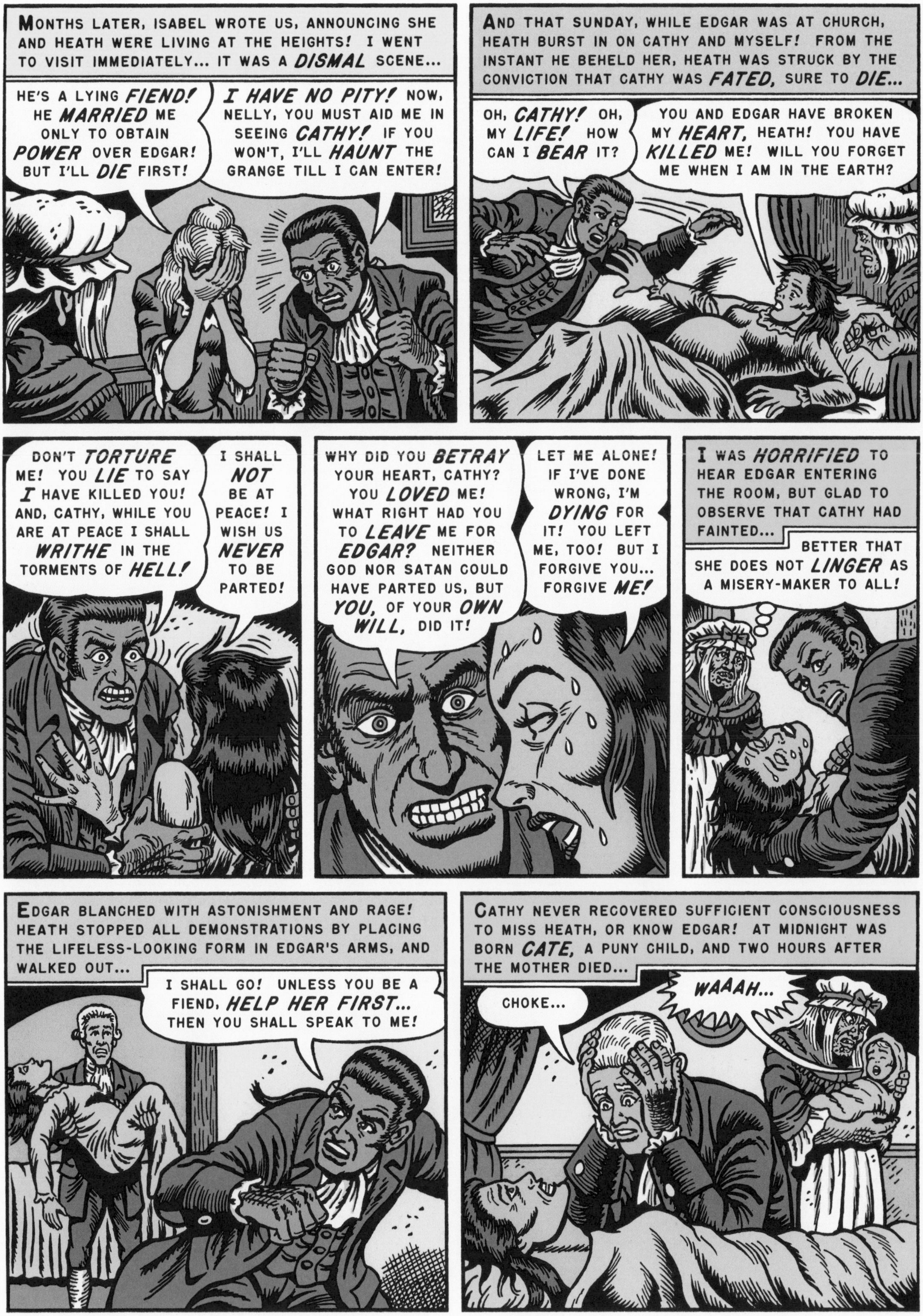
MONTHS LATER, ISABEL WROTE US, ANNOUNCING SHE AND HEATH WERE LIVING AT THE HEIGHTS! I WENT TO VISIT IMMEDIATELY... IT WAS A DISMAL SCENE...
HE'S A LYING FIEND! HE MARRIED ME ONLY TO OBTAIN POWER OVER EDGAR! BUT I'LL DIE FIRST!
I HAVE NO PITY! NOW, NELLY, YOU MUST AID ME IN SEEING CATHY! IF YOU WON'T, I'LL HAUNT THE GRANGE TILL I CAN ENTER!
AND THAT SUNDAY, WHILE EDGAR WAS AT CHURCH, HEATH BURST IN ON CATHY AND MYSELF! FROM THE INSTANT HE BEHELD HER, HEATH WAS STRUCK BY THE CONVICTION THAT CATHY WAS FATED, SURE TO DIE...
OH, CATHY! OH, MY LIFE! HOW CAN I BEAR IT?
YOU AND EDGAR HAVE BROKEN MY HEART, HEATH! YOU HAVE KILLED ME! WILL YOU FORGET ME WHEN I AM IN THE EARTH?
DON'T TORTURE ME! YOU LIE TO SAY I HAVE KILLED YOU! AND, CATHY, WHILE YOU ARE AT PEACE I SHALL WRITHE IN THE TORMENTS OF HELL!
I SHALL NOT BE AT PEACE! I WISH US NEVER TO BE PARTED!
WHY DID YOU BETRAY YOUR HEART, CATHY? YOU LOVED ME! WHAT RIGHT HAD YOU TO LEAVE ME FOR EDGAR? NEITHER GOD NOR SATAN COULD HAVE PARTED US, BUT YOU, OF YOUR OWN WILL, DID IT!
LET ME ALONE! IF I'VE DONE WRONG, I'M DYING FOR IT! YOU LEFT ME, TOO! BUT I FORGIVE YOU... FORGIVE ME!
I WAS HORRIFIED TO HEAR EDGAR ENTERING THE ROOM, BUT GLAD TO OBSERVE THAT CATHY HAD FAINTED...
BETTER THAT SHE DOES NOT LINGER AS A MISERY-MAKER TO ALL!
EDGAR BLANCHED WITH ASTONISHMENT AND RAGE! HEATH STOPPED ALL DEMONSTRATIONS BY PLACING THE LIFELESS-LOOKING FORM IN EDGAR'S ARMS, AND WALKED OUT...
I SHALL GO! UNLESS YOU BE A FIEND, HELP HER FIRST... THEN YOU SHALL SPEAK TO ME!
CATHY NEVER RECOVERED SUFFICIENT CONSCIOUSNESS TO MISS HEATH, OR KNOW EDGAR! AT MIDNIGHT WAS BORN CATE, A PUNY CHILD, AND TWO HOURS AFTER THE MOTHER DIED...
CHOKE...
WAAAH...

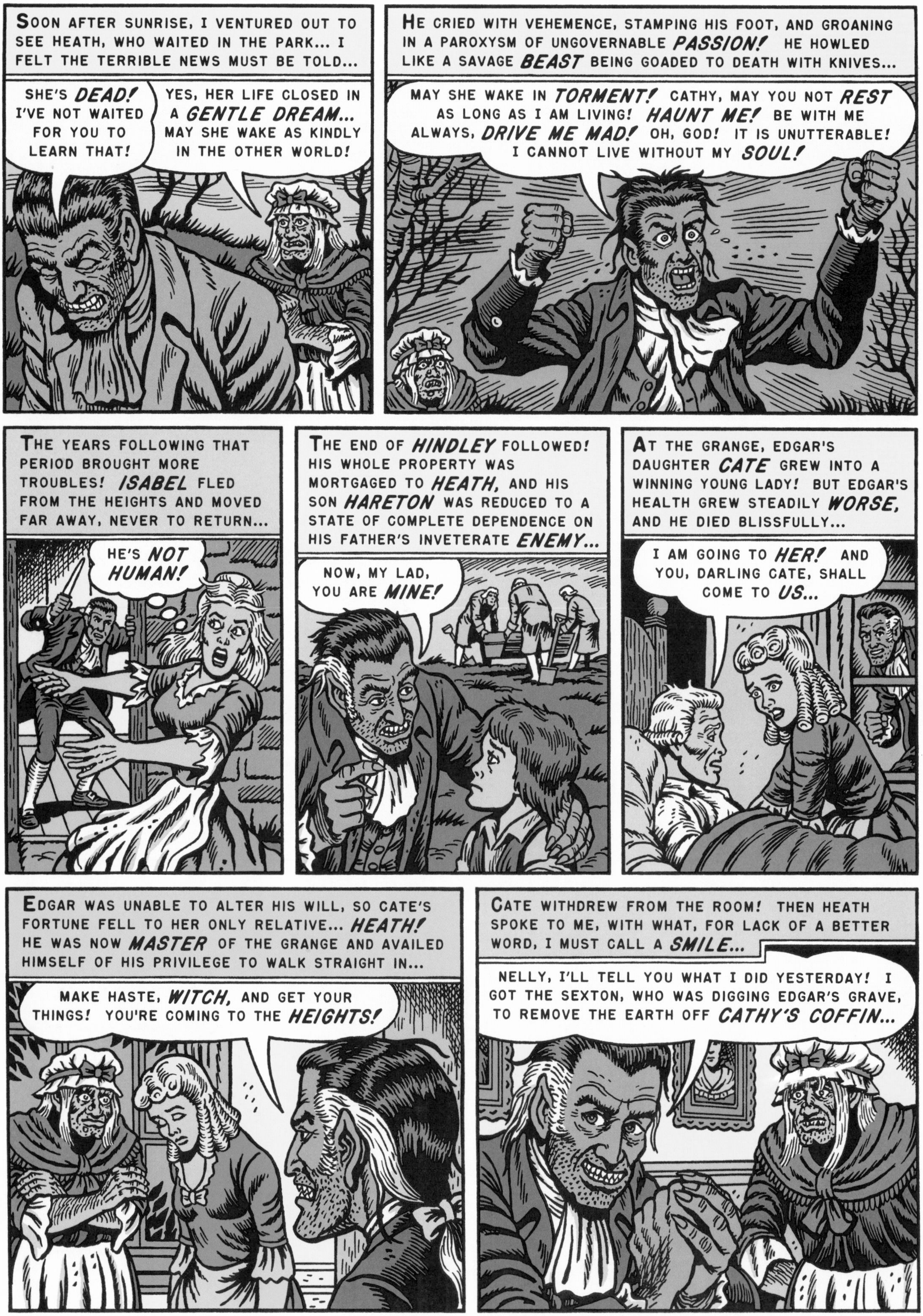

SOON AFTER SUNRISE, I VENTURED OUT TO SEE HEATH, WHO WAITED IN THE PARK... I FELT THE TERRIBLE NEWS MUST BE TOLD...
SHE'S DEAD! I'VE NOT WAITED FOR YOU TO LEARN THAT!
YES, HER LIFE CLOSED IN A GENTLE DREAM... MAY SHE WAKE AS KINDLY IN THE OTHER WORLD!
HE CRIED WITH VEHEMENCE, STAMPING HIS FOOT, AND GROANING IN A PAROXYSM OF UNGOVERNABLE PASSION! HE HOWLED LIKE A SAVAGE BEAST BEING GOADED TO DEATH WITH KNIVES...
MAY SHE WAKE IN TORMENT! CATHY, MAY YOU NOT REST AS LONG AS I AM LIVING! HAUNT ME! BE WITH ME ALWAYS, DRIVE ME MAD! OH, GOD! IT IS UNUTTERABLE! I CANNOT LIVE WITHOUT MY SOUL!
THE YEARS FOLLOWING THAT PERIOD BROUGHT MORE TROUBLES! ISABEL FLED FROM THE HEIGHTS AND MOVED FAR AWAY, NEVER TO RETURN...
HE'S NOT HUMAN!
THE END OF HINDLEY FOLLOWED! HIS WHOLE PROPERTY WAS MORTGAGED TO HEATH, AND HIS SON HARETON WAS REDUCED TO A STATE OF COMPLETE DEPENDENCE ON HIS FATHER'S INVETERATE ENEMY...
NOW, MY LAD, YOU ARE MINE!
AT THE GRANGE, EDGAR'S DAUGHTER CATE GREW INTO A WINNING YOUNG LADY! BUT EDGAR'S HEALTH GREW STEADILY WORSE, AND HE DIED BLISSFULLY...
I AM GOING TO HER! AND YOU, DARLING CATE, SHALL COME TO US...
EDGAR WAS UNABLE TO ALTER HIS WILL, SO CATE'S FORTUNE FELL TO HER ONLY RELATIVE... HEATH! HE WAS NOW MASTER OF THE GRANGE AND AVAILED HIMSELF OF HIS PRIVILEGE TO WALK STRAIGHT IN...
MAKE HASTE, WITCH, AND GET YOUR THINGS! YOU'RE COMING TO THE HEIGHTS!
CATE WITHDREW FROM THE ROOM! THEN HEATH SPOKE TO ME, WITH WHAT, FOR LACK OF A BETTER WORD, I MUST CALL A SMILE...
NELLY, I'LL TELL YOU WHAT I DID YESTERDAY! I GOT THE SEXTON, WHO WAS DIGGING EDGAR'S GRAVE, TO REMOVE THE EARTH OFF CATHY'S COFFIN...

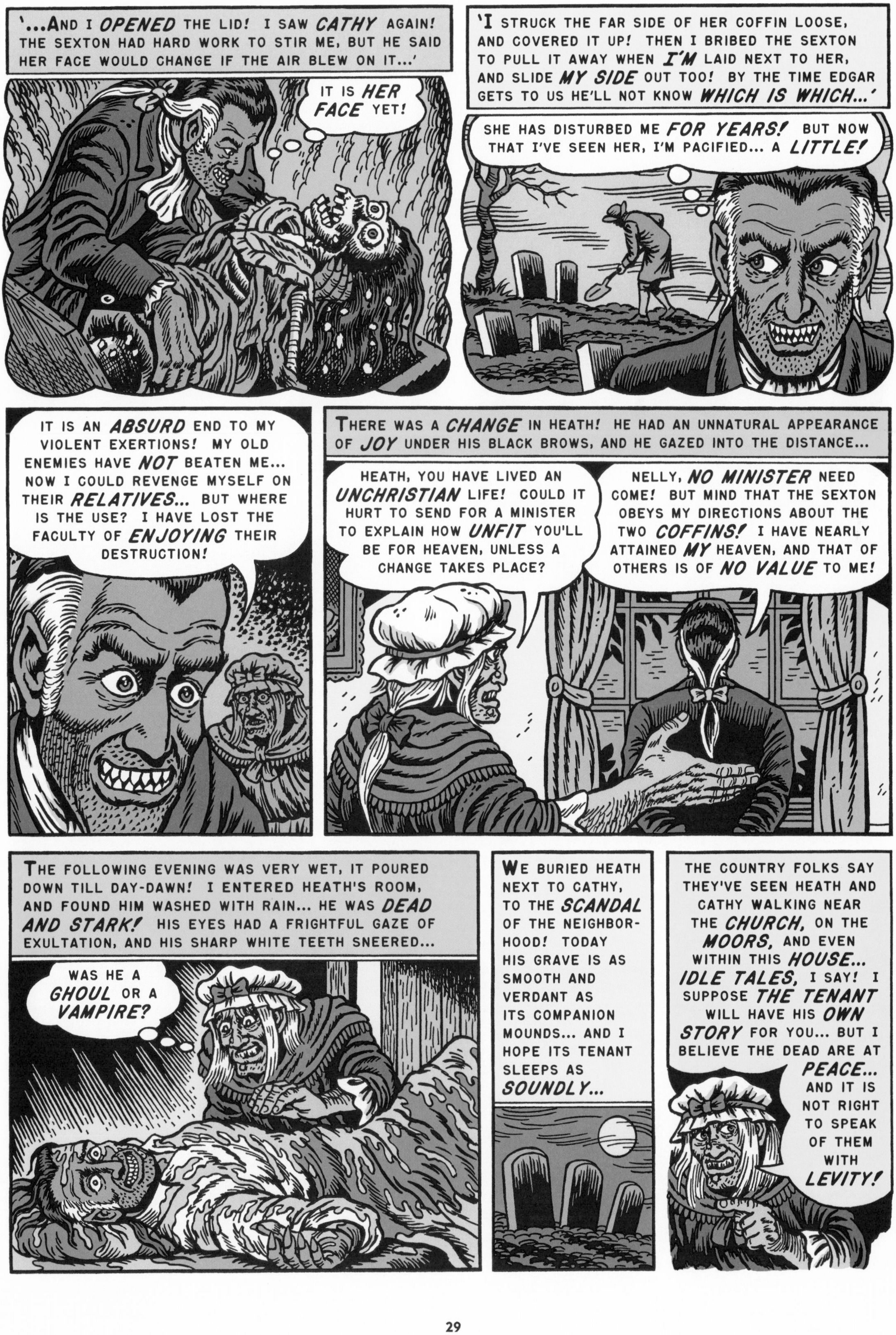
'...AND I OPENED THE LID! I SAW CATHY AGAIN! THE SEXTON HAD HARD WORK TO STIR ME, BUT HE SAID HER FACE WOULD CHANGE IF THE AIR BLEW ON IT...'
IT IS HER FACE YET!
'I STRUCK THE FAR SIDE OF HER COFFIN LOOSE, AND COVERED IT UP! THEN I BRIBED THE SEXTON TO PULL IT AWAY WHEN I'M LAID NEXT TO HER, AND SLIDE MY SIDE OUT TOO! BY THE TIME EDGAR GETS TO US HE'LL NOT KNOW WHICH IS WHICH...'
SHE HAS DISTURBED ME FOR YEARS! BUT NOW THAT I'VE SEEN HER, I'M PACIFIED... A LITTLE!
IT IS AN ABSURD END TO MY VIOLENT EXERTIONS! MY OLD ENEMIES HAVE NOT BEATEN ME... NOW I COULD REVENGE MYSELF ON THEIR RELATIVES... BUT WHERE IS THE USE? I HAVE LOST THE FACULTY OF ENJOYING THEIR DESTRUCTION!
THERE WAS A CHANGE IN HEATH! HE HAD AN UNNATURAL APPEARANCE OF JOY UNDER HIS BLACK BROWS, AND HE GAZED INTO THE DISTANCE...
HEATH, YOU HAVE LIVED AN UNCHRISTIAN LIFE! COULD IT HURT TO SEND FOR A MINISTER TO EXPLAIN HOW UNFIT YOU'LL BE FOR HEAVEN, UNLESS A CHANGE TAKES PLACE?
NELLY, NO MINISTER NEED COME! BUT MIND THAT THE SEXTON OBEYS MY DIRECTIONS ABOUT THE TWO COFFINS! I HAVE NEARLY ATTAINED MY HEAVEN, AND THAT OF OTHERS IS OF NO VALUE TO ME!
THE FOLLOWING EVENING WAS VERY WET, IT POURED DOWN TILL DAY-DAWN! I ENTERED HEATH'S ROOM, AND FOUND HIM WASHED WITH RAIN... HE WAS DEAD AND STARK! HIS EYES HAD A FRIGHTFUL GAZE OF EXULTATION, AND HIS SHARP WHITE TEETH SNEERED...
WAS HE A GHOUL OR A VAMPIRE?
WE BURIED HEATH NEXT TO CATHY, TO THE SCANDAL OF THE NEIGHBOR-HOOD! TODAY HIS GRAVE IS AS SMOOTH AND VERDANT AS ITS COMPANION MOUNDS... AND I HOPE ITS TENANT SLEEPS AS SOUNDLY...
THE COUNTRY FOLKS SAY THEY'VE SEEN HEATH AND CATHY WALKING NEAR THE CHURCH, ON THE MOORS, AND EVEN WITHIN THIS HOUSE... IDLE TALES, I SAY! I SUPPOSE THE TENANT WILL HAVE HIS OWN STORY FOR YOU... BUT I BELIEVE THE DEAD ARE AT PEACE... AND IT IS NOT RIGHT TO SPEAK OF THEM WITH LEVITY!

Masterpiece QUERIES

Have a question about a story? Send your letters to: Professor Scholar c/o the publisher.

Dear Professor S.,

In BLOND EVE, Adam has a funny way of carrying apples on his arms. Why does he do that? — J. Bois, Cambridgeshire, ENG

There is a similar food-balancing technique used in cartoonist Chic Young's 1930 newspaper strip, which stars America's favorite golden-haired housewife and her overworked spouse. One will recognize several points of comparison between those two well-meaning mortals and the couple described in the first story of Genesis. In particular, the means by which the modern-day harried husband conveys sandwich ingredients to his kitchen table unconsciously evokes the way individuals must juggle free will and their duties to the creator in the Judeo-Christian scriptures. His technique also saves many trips to the refrigerator.

Dear Prof.,

Are the INFERNO JOE prizes still available?

— Gio Boccaccio, Tuscany, IT

According to Dante Alighieri, author of the 1321 Commedia, the prizes will be around for eternity. In this way, they are reminiscent of the candy products created by the Topps Company since the mid-twentieth century. In this writer's experience, novelty bubblegum has seemed utterly impervious to age, foul weather conditions, and occasionally, human mastication. Thus, the 1/2" tall panels by the 1950's gum-wrapper-artist Wesley Morse were a natural influence on the tone and style of this story's gag-cantos.

Hello P.S.,

Jon Faustus is always bossing MEPHISTOFIELD around, and yet Meph is really in control the whole time. What's going on here? — Val Simmes, London, ENG

Apparently you've never had a cat. The relationship of mortal to demon is remarkably similar to that of the main characters of graphic humorist Jim Davis' sprawling tabby saga (1978 - present), wherein the lasagna-providing human is ultimately at the mercy of his lasagna-loving pet. Whether or not the dramatist Christopher Marlowe, author of the 1592 version, was personally at the mercy of such a kitty remains unknown.

To the Professor,

In MAC WORTH, why would Mac listen to Mrs. M.'s terrible advice? — Henry C., London, ENG

Perhaps Mac was the wrong man for the job. He couldn't "screw [his] courage to the sticking-place," as the poet William

Shakespeare expressed it in his Scottish play, circa 1607. The personality of Mrs. M. is reminiscent of the titular character of a 1940 dramatic comic strip, produced for many years by the team of writer Allen Sanders and artist Ken Ernst. That cartoon star is a kindly and perceptive busybody, whose advice is consistently, and startlingly, very effective and generally embraced by her many friends and relations. In our story, Mac somewhat resembles a fictional medical doctor (who is also himself the eponymous star of another serialized strip, realized in 1948 by the team of Dal Curtis, Marvin Bradley, and Frank Edgington). That doctor was far more effective using knives to perform surgery than he ever would be to commit murder.

Dear Prof. S.,

I was charmed by CANDIGGY! The little guy never gives up, no matter what happens! Any chance we'll be seeing him and reading his feel-good slogans on a series of greeting cards?

— J. de Fleury, Paris, FR

While Candiggy somewhat evokes Tom Wilson's similarly-statured, heartwarming creation, a star of cartoon panels and cards since 1968, Candiggy's experiences somewhat differ in their intensity. Also, it's unlikely that the aphorisms of the author Voltaire (particularly those found in his 1759 satire) will be exchanged during most American holidays.

Dear Professor Scholar,

THE CRYPT OF BRONTË ended really quickly, before all the loose ends were tied up. What happened to young Cate and Hareton? — Currer B., Yorkshire, ENG

At the end of Emily Brontë's 1847 Gothic-inspired novel, Cate and Hareton are happily preparing for their marriage. However, their joy didn't serve the purposes of our tale of revenge. If you are familiar with the 1950's graphic horror narratives of Al Feldstein and Jack Davis that inspired this retelling, you will recall that those gruesome morality tales always emphasized wickedness (even when thwarted) over goodness (which was considered tedious). Besides, as those stories were eight pages or less, it was vital to carefully choose the only most memorable moments of the novel's thirty years of events: the punching, the dying, the apple-sauce-tossing, the violent kissing, and the grave-tampering.

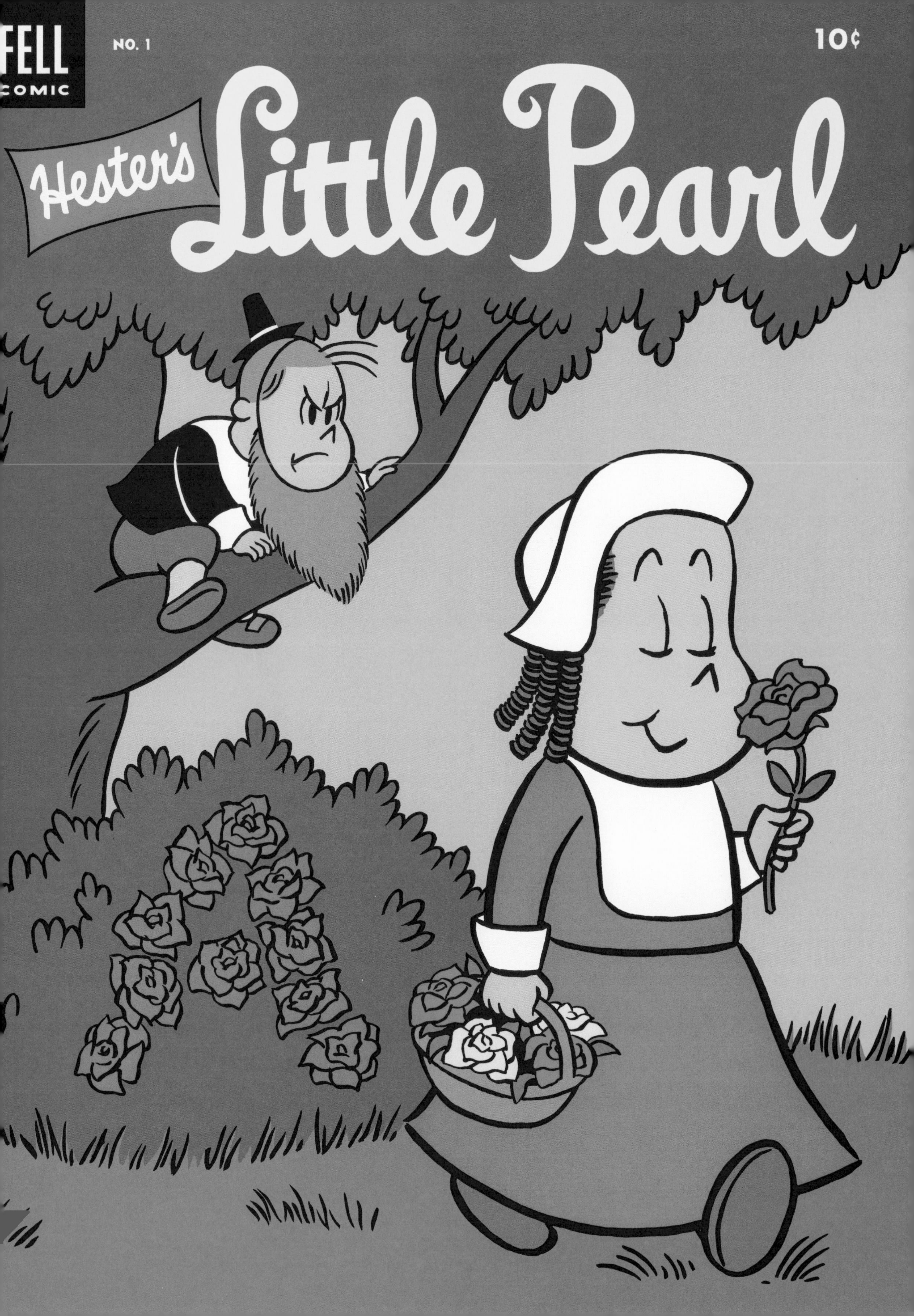
DELL COMIC
NO. 1
10¢
Hester's
Little Pearl

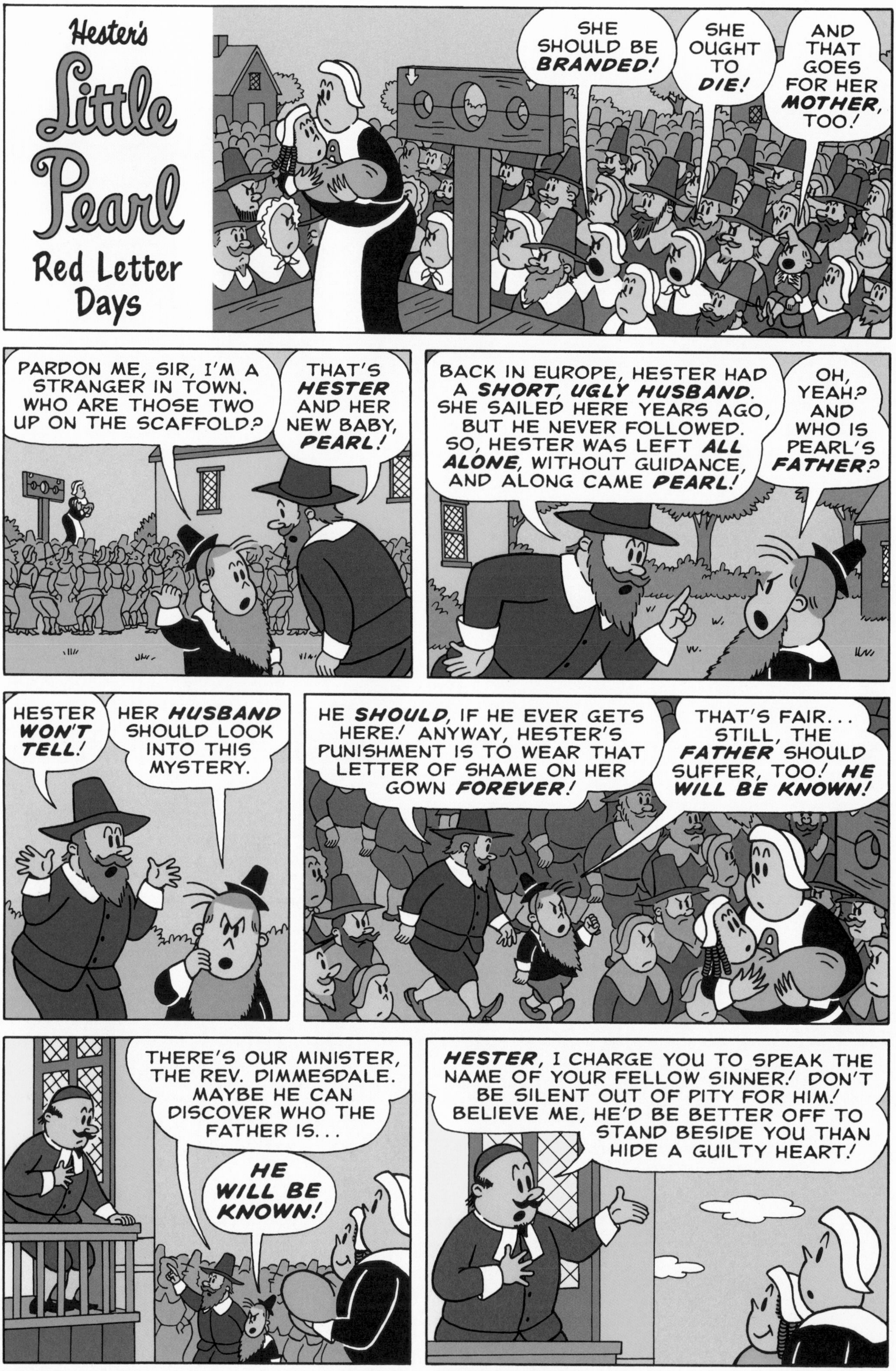

Hester's Little Pearl
Red Letter Days
SHE SHOULD BE BRANDED!
SHE OUGHT TO DIE!
AND THAT GOES FOR HER MOTHER, TOO!
PARDON ME, SIR, I'M A STRANGER IN TOWN. WHO ARE THOSE TWO UP ON THE SCAFFOLD?
THAT'S HESTER AND HER NEW BABY, PEARL!
BACK IN EUROPE, HESTER HAD A SHORT, UGLY HUSBAND. SHE SAILED HERE YEARS AGO, BUT HE NEVER FOLLOWED. SO, HESTER WAS LEFT ALL ALONE, WITHOUT GUIDANCE, AND ALONG CAME PEARL!
OH, YEAH? AND WHO IS PEARL'S FATHER?
HESTER WON'T TELL!
HER HUSBAND SHOULD LOOK INTO THIS MYSTERY.
HE SHOULD, IF HE EVER GETS HERE! ANYWAY, HESTER'S PUNISHMENT IS TO WEAR THAT LETTER OF SHAME ON HER GOWN FOREVER!
THAT'S FAIR... STILL, THE FATHER SHOULD SUFFER, TOO! HE WILL BE KNOWN!
THERE'S OUR MINISTER, THE REV. DIMMESDALE. MAYBE HE CAN DISCOVER WHO THE FATHER IS...
HE WILL BE KNOWN!
HESTER, I CHARGE YOU TO SPEAK THE NAME OF YOUR FELLOW SINNER! DON'T BE SILENT OUT OF PITY FOR HIM! BELIEVE ME, HE'D BE BETTER OFF TO STAND BESIDE YOU THAN HIDE A GUILTY HEART!

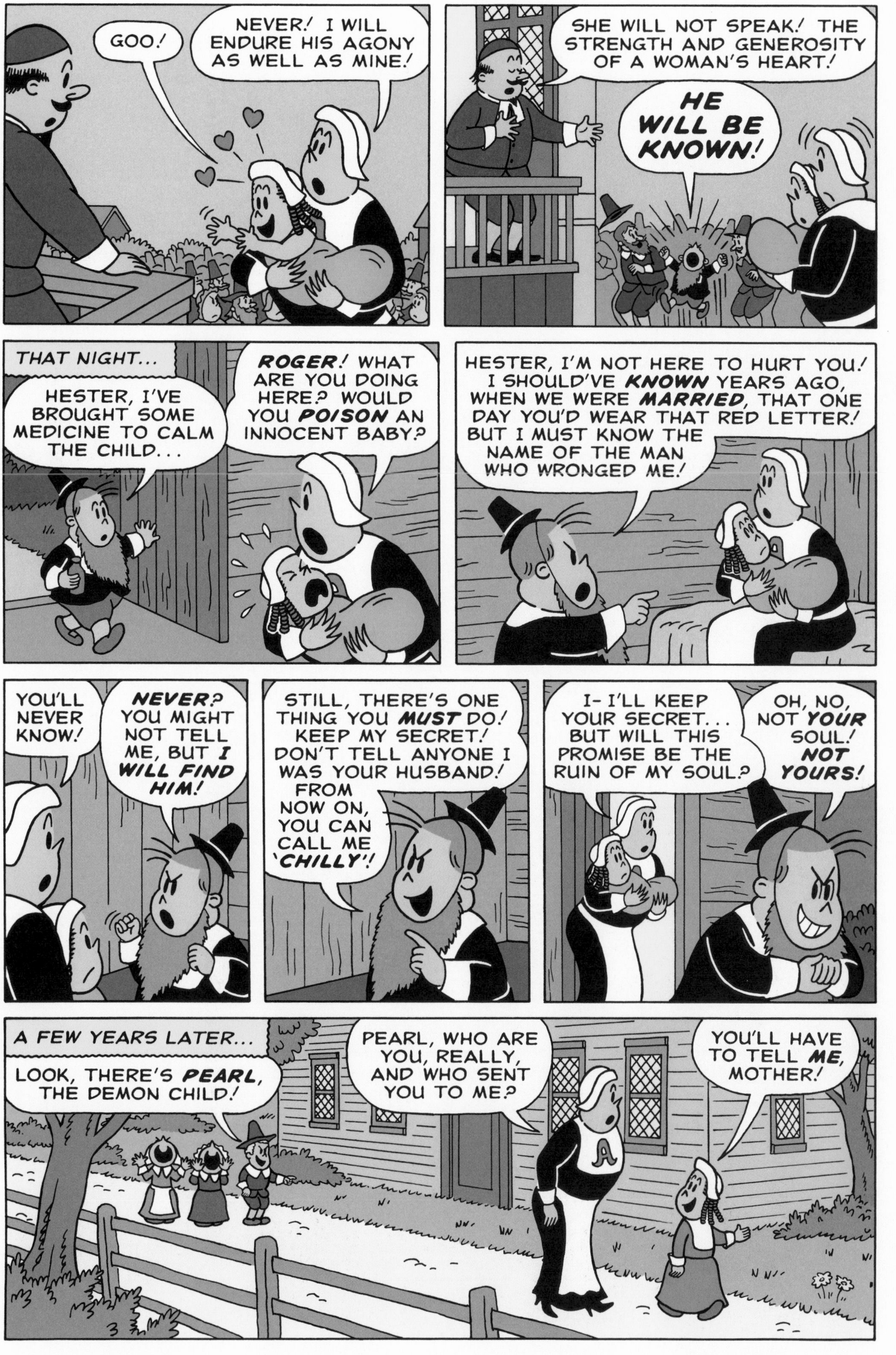
GOO!
NEVER! I WILL ENDURE HIS AGONY AS WELL AS MINE!
SHE WILL NOT SPEAK! THE STRENGTH AND GENEROSITY OF A WOMAN'S HEART!
HE WILL BE KNOWN!
THAT NIGHT...
HESTER, I'VE BROUGHT SOME MEDICINE TO CALM THE CHILD...
ROGER! WHAT ARE YOU DOING HERE? WOULD YOU POISON AN INNOCENT BABY?
HESTER, I'M NOT HERE TO HURT YOU! I SHOULD'VE KNOWN YEARS AGO, WHEN WE WERE MARRIED, THAT ONE DAY YOU'D WEAR THAT RED LETTER! BUT I MUST KNOW THE NAME OF THE MAN WHO WRONGED ME!
YOU'LL NEVER KNOW!
NEVER? YOU MIGHT NOT TELL ME, BUT I WILL FIND HIM!
STILL, THERE'S ONE THING YOU MUST DO! KEEP MY SECRET! DON'T TELL ANYONE I WAS YOUR HUSBAND! FROM NOW ON, YOU CAN CALL ME 'CHILLY'!
I- I'LL KEEP YOUR SECRET... BUT WILL THIS PROMISE BE THE RUIN OF MY SOUL?
OH, NO, NOT YOUR SOUL! NOT YOURS!
A FEW YEARS LATER...
LOOK, THERE'S PEARL, THE DEMON CHILD!
PEARL, WHO ARE YOU, REALLY, AND WHO SENT YOU TO ME?
YOU'LL HAVE TO TELL ME, MOTHER!
A

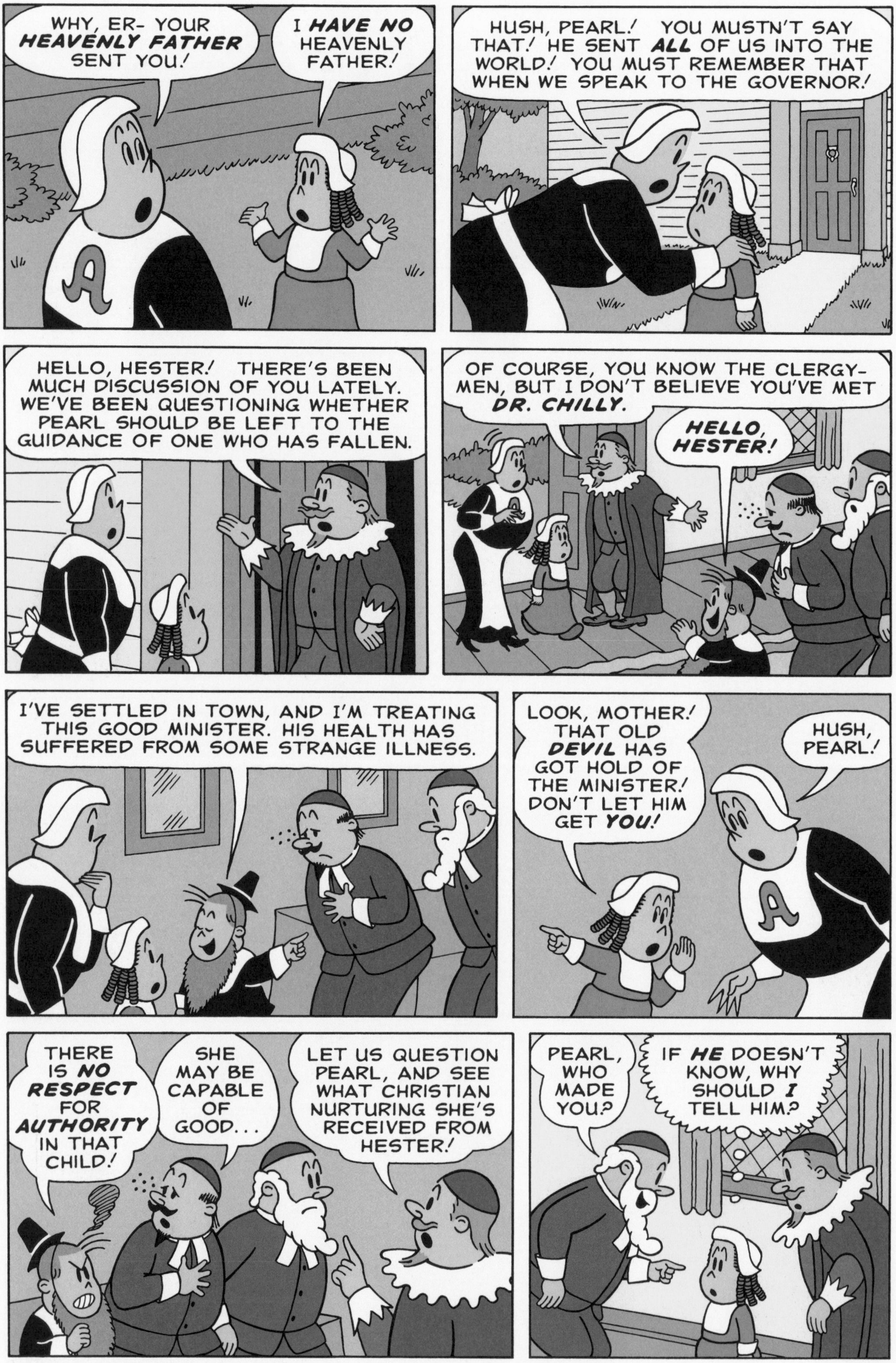
WHY, ER- YOUR **HEAVENLY FATHER** SENT YOU!
I **HAVE NO** HEAVENLY FATHER!
HUSH, PEARL! YOU MUSTN'T SAY THAT! HE SENT **ALL** OF US INTO THE WORLD! YOU MUST REMEMBER THAT WHEN WE SPEAK TO THE GOVERNOR!
HELLO, HESTER! THERE'S BEEN MUCH DISCUSSION OF YOU LATELY. WE'VE BEEN QUESTIONING WHETHER PEARL SHOULD BE LEFT TO THE GUIDANCE OF ONE WHO HAS FALLEN.
OF COURSE, YOU KNOW THE CLERGYMEN, BUT I DON'T BELIEVE YOU'VE MET **DR. CHILLY**.
HELLO, HESTER!
I'VE SETTLED IN TOWN, AND I'M TREATING THIS GOOD MINISTER. HIS HEALTH HAS SUFFERED FROM SOME STRANGE ILLNESS.
LOOK, MOTHER! THAT OLD **DEVIL** HAS GOT HOLD OF THE MINISTER! DON'T LET HIM GET **YOU**!
HUSH, PEARL!
THERE IS **NO RESPECT** FOR **AUTHORITY** IN THAT CHILD!
SHE MAY BE CAPABLE OF GOOD...
LET US QUESTION PEARL, AND SEE WHAT CHRISTIAN NURTURING SHE'S RECEIVED FROM HESTER!
PEARL, WHO MADE YOU?
IF **HE** DOESN'T KNOW, WHY SHOULD **I** TELL HIM?

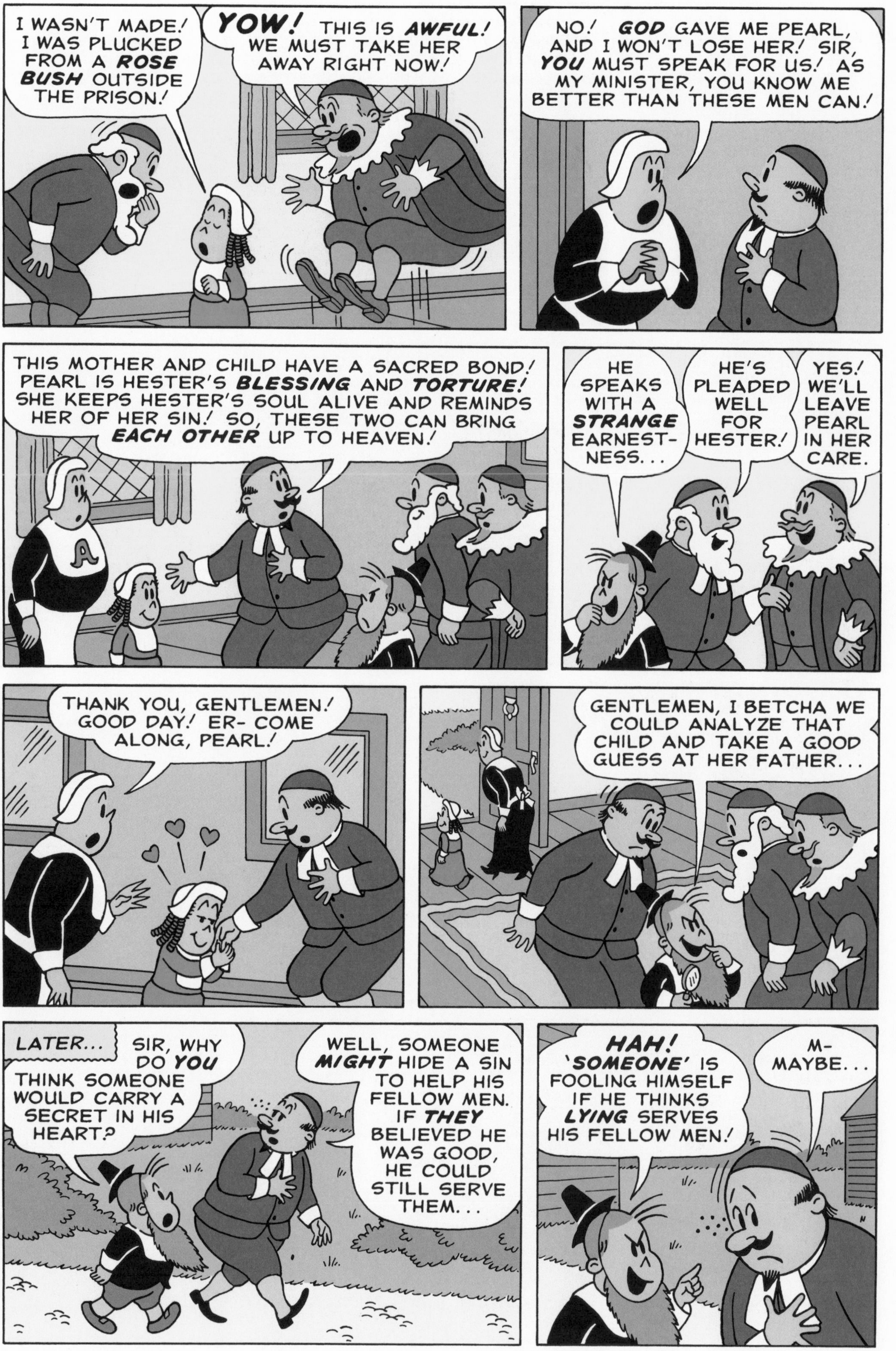
I WASN'T MADE! I WAS PLUCKED FROM A ROSE BUSH OUTSIDE THE PRISON!
YOW! THIS IS AWFUL! WE MUST TAKE HER AWAY RIGHT NOW!
NO! GOD GAVE ME PEARL, AND I WON'T LOSE HER! SIR, YOU MUST SPEAK FOR US! AS MY MINISTER, YOU KNOW ME BETTER THAN THESE MEN CAN!
THIS MOTHER AND CHILD HAVE A SACRED BOND! PEARL IS HESTER'S BLESSING AND TORTURE! SHE KEEPS HESTER'S SOUL ALIVE AND REMINDS HER OF HER SIN! SO, THESE TWO CAN BRING EACH OTHER UP TO HEAVEN!
HE SPEAKS WITH A STRANGE EARNESTNESS...
HE'S PLEADED WELL FOR HESTER!
YES! WE'LL LEAVE PEARL IN HER CARE.
THANK YOU, GENTLEMEN! GOOD DAY! ER- COME ALONG, PEARL!
GENTLEMEN, I BETCHA WE COULD ANALYZE THAT CHILD AND TAKE A GOOD GUESS AT HER FATHER...
LATER...
SIR, WHY DO YOU THINK SOMEONE WOULD CARRY A SECRET IN HIS HEART?
WELL, SOMEONE MIGHT HIDE A SIN TO HELP HIS FELLOW MEN. IF THEY BELIEVED HE WAS GOOD, HE COULD STILL SERVE THEM...
HAH! 'SOMEONE' IS FOOLING HIMSELF IF HE THINKS LYING SERVES HIS FELLOW MEN!
M- MAYBE...

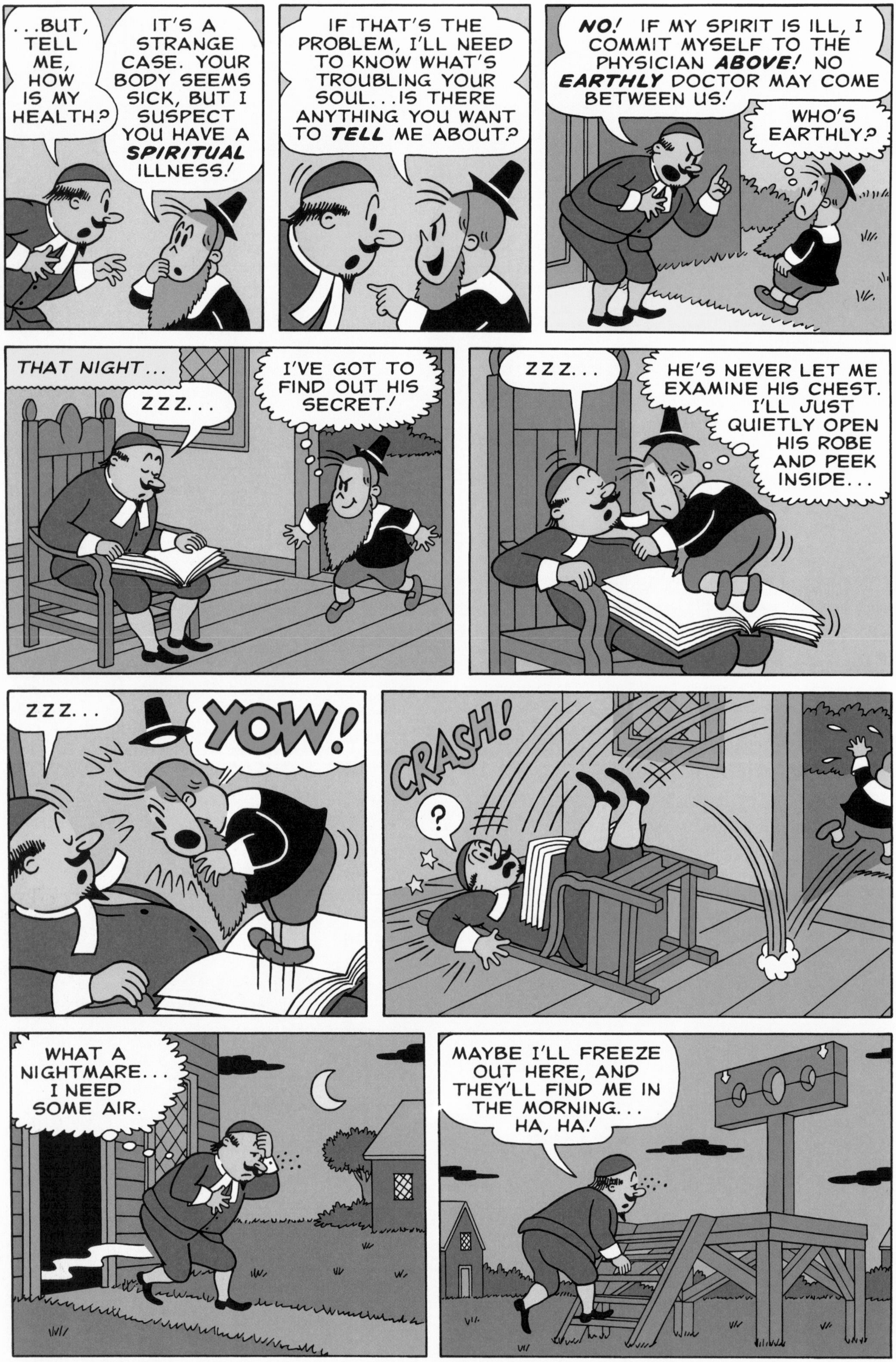
...BUT, TELL ME, HOW IS MY HEALTH?
IT'S A STRANGE CASE. YOUR BODY SEEMS SICK, BUT I SUSPECT YOU HAVE A SPIRITUAL ILLNESS!
IF THAT'S THE PROBLEM, I'LL NEED TO KNOW WHAT'S TROUBLING YOUR SOUL...IS THERE ANYTHING YOU WANT TO TELL ME ABOUT?
NO! IF MY SPIRIT IS ILL, I COMMIT MYSELF TO THE PHYSICIAN ABOVE! NO EARTHLY DOCTOR MAY COME BETWEEN US!
WHO'S EARTHLY?
THAT NIGHT...
ZZZ...
I'VE GOT TO FIND OUT HIS SECRET!
ZZZ...
HE'S NEVER LET ME EXAMINE HIS CHEST. I'LL JUST QUIETLY OPEN HIS ROBE AND PEEK INSIDE...
ZZZ...
YOW!
CRASH!
?
WHAT A NIGHTMARE... I NEED SOME AIR.
MAYBE I'LL FREEZE OUT HERE, AND THEY'LL FIND ME IN THE MORNING... HA, HA!

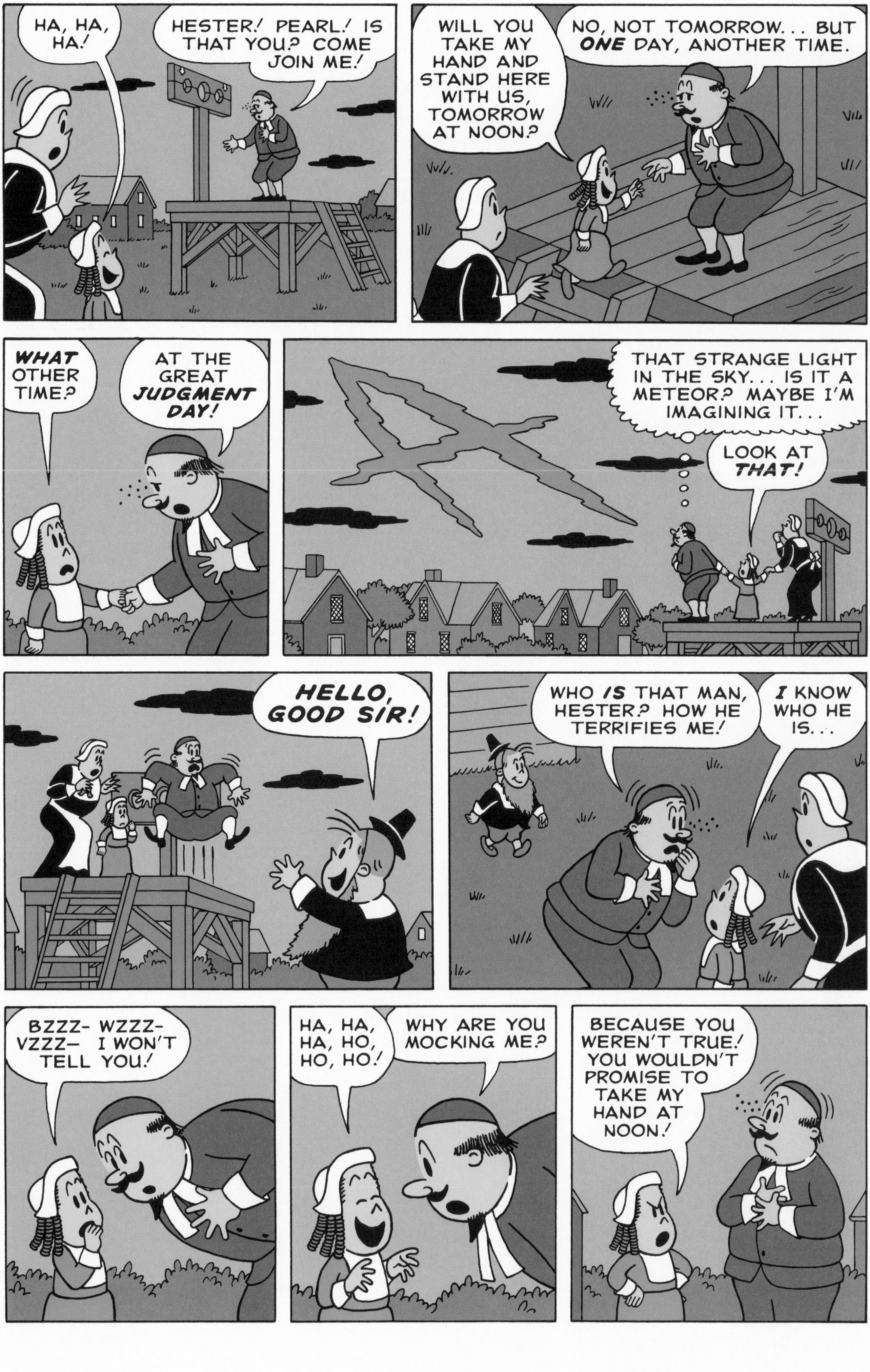

HA, HA, HA!
HESTER! PEARL! IS THAT YOU? COME JOIN ME!
WILL YOU TAKE MY HAND AND STAND HERE WITH US, TOMORROW AT NOON?
NO, NOT TOMORROW... BUT ONE DAY, ANOTHER TIME.
WHAT OTHER TIME?
AT THE GREAT JUDGMENT DAY!
THAT STRANGE LIGHT IN THE SKY... IS IT A METEOR? MAYBE I'M IMAGINING IT...
LOOK AT THAT!
HELLO, GOOD SIR!
WHO IS THAT MAN, HESTER? HOW HE TERRIFIES ME!
I KNOW WHO HE IS...
BZZZ- WZZZ- VZZZ- I WON'T TELL YOU!
HA, HA, HA, HO, HO, HO!
WHY ARE YOU MOCKING ME?
BECAUSE YOU WEREN'T TRUE! YOU WOULDN'T PROMISE TO TAKE MY HAND AT NOON!

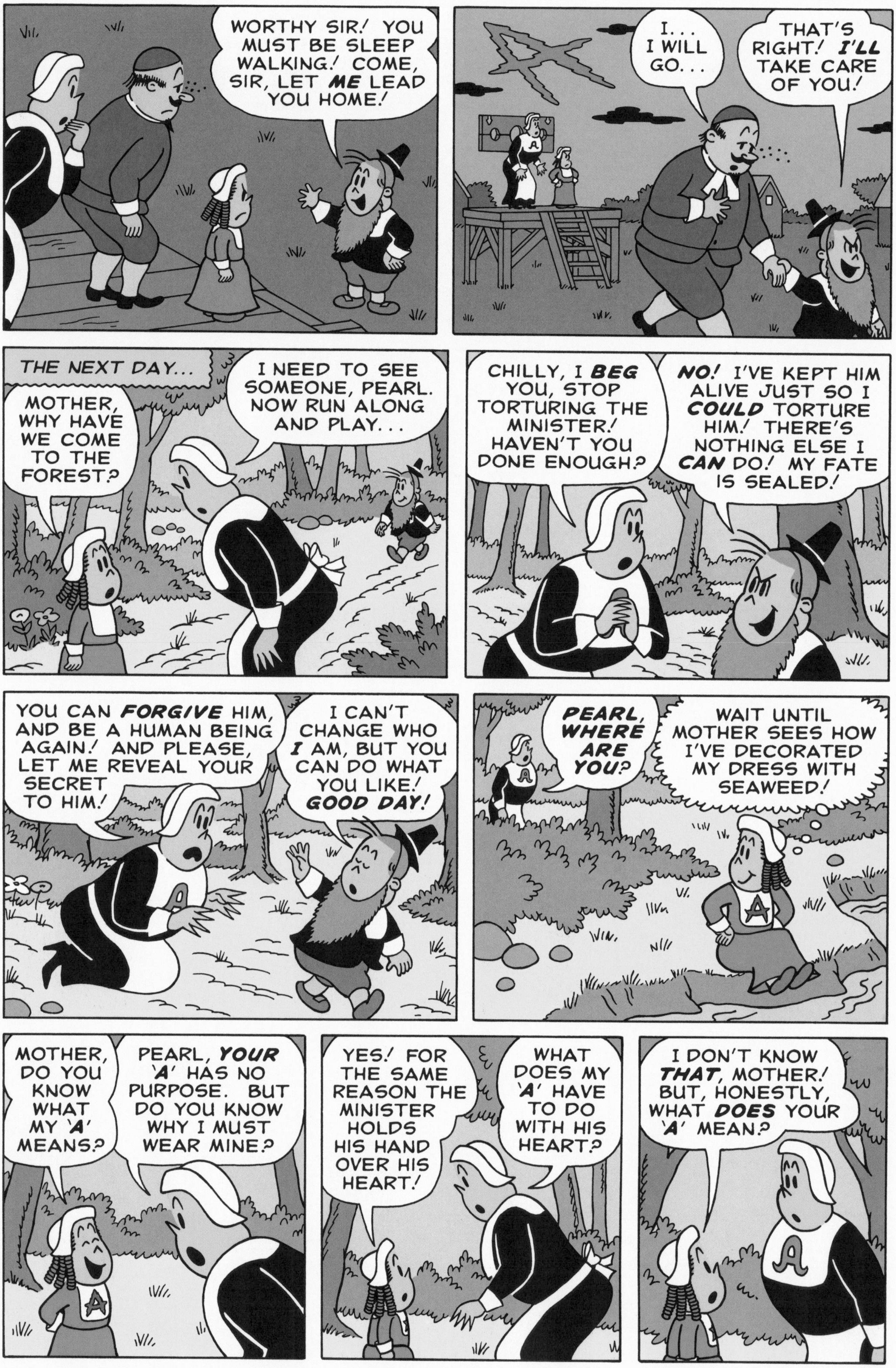
WORTHY SIR! YOU MUST BE SLEEP WALKING! COME, SIR, LET ME LEAD YOU HOME!
I... I WILL GO...
THAT'S RIGHT! I'LL TAKE CARE OF YOU!
THE NEXT DAY...
MOTHER, WHY HAVE WE COME TO THE FOREST?
I NEED TO SEE SOMEONE, PEARL. NOW RUN ALONG AND PLAY...
CHILLY, I BEG YOU, STOP TORTURING THE MINISTER! HAVEN'T YOU DONE ENOUGH?
NO! I'VE KEPT HIM ALIVE JUST SO I COULD TORTURE HIM! THERE'S NOTHING ELSE I CAN DO! MY FATE IS SEALED!
YOU CAN FORGIVE HIM, AND BE A HUMAN BEING AGAIN! AND PLEASE, LET ME REVEAL YOUR SECRET TO HIM!
I CAN'T CHANGE WHO I AM, BUT YOU CAN DO WHAT YOU LIKE! GOOD DAY!
PEARL, WHERE ARE YOU?
WAIT UNTIL MOTHER SEES HOW I'VE DECORATED MY DRESS WITH SEAWEED!
MOTHER, DO YOU KNOW WHAT MY 'A' MEANS?
PEARL, YOUR 'A' HAS NO PURPOSE. BUT DO YOU KNOW WHY I MUST WEAR MINE?
YES! FOR THE SAME REASON THE MINISTER HOLDS HIS HAND OVER HIS HEART!
WHAT DOES MY 'A' HAVE TO DO WITH HIS HEART?
I DON'T KNOW THAT, MOTHER! BUT, HONESTLY, WHAT DOES YOUR 'A' MEAN?

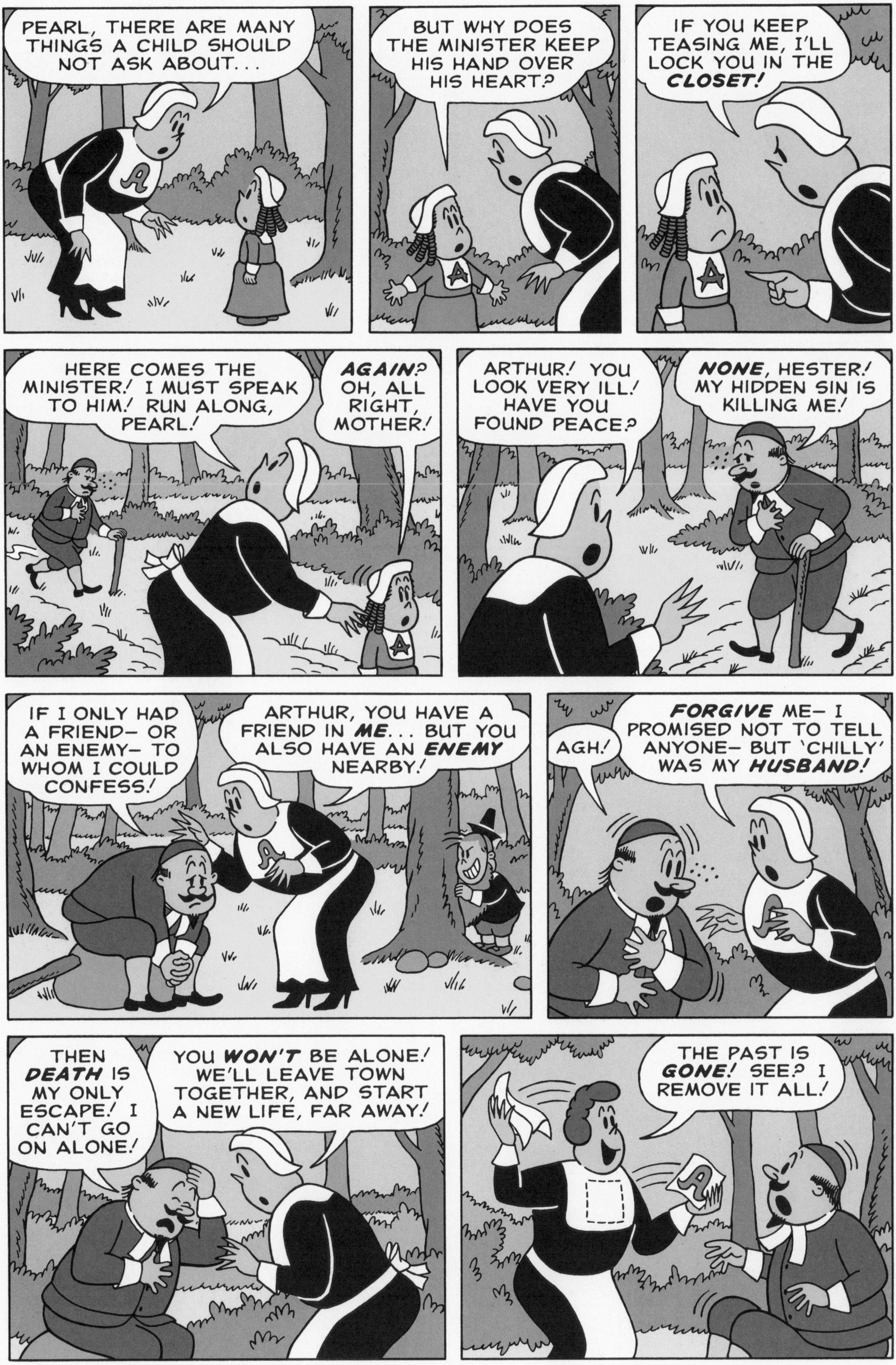
PEARL, THERE ARE MANY THINGS A CHILD SHOULD NOT ASK ABOUT...
BUT WHY DOES THE MINISTER KEEP HIS HAND OVER HIS HEART?
IF YOU KEEP TEASING ME, I'LL LOCK YOU IN THE CLOSET!
HERE COMES THE MINISTER! I MUST SPEAK TO HIM! RUN ALONG, PEARL!
AGAIN? OH, ALL RIGHT, MOTHER!
ARTHUR! YOU LOOK VERY ILL! HAVE YOU FOUND PEACE?
NONE, HESTER! MY HIDDEN SIN IS KILLING ME!
IF I ONLY HAD A FRIEND– OR AN ENEMY– TO WHOM I COULD CONFESS!
ARTHUR, YOU HAVE A FRIEND IN ME... BUT YOU ALSO HAVE AN ENEMY NEARBY!
FORGIVE ME– I PROMISED NOT TO TELL ANYONE– BUT 'CHILLY' WAS MY HUSBAND!
AGH!
THEN DEATH IS MY ONLY ESCAPE! I CAN'T GO ON ALONE!
YOU WON'T BE ALONE! WE'LL LEAVE TOWN TOGETHER, AND START A NEW LIFE, FAR AWAY!
THE PAST IS GONE! SEE? I REMOVE IT ALL!

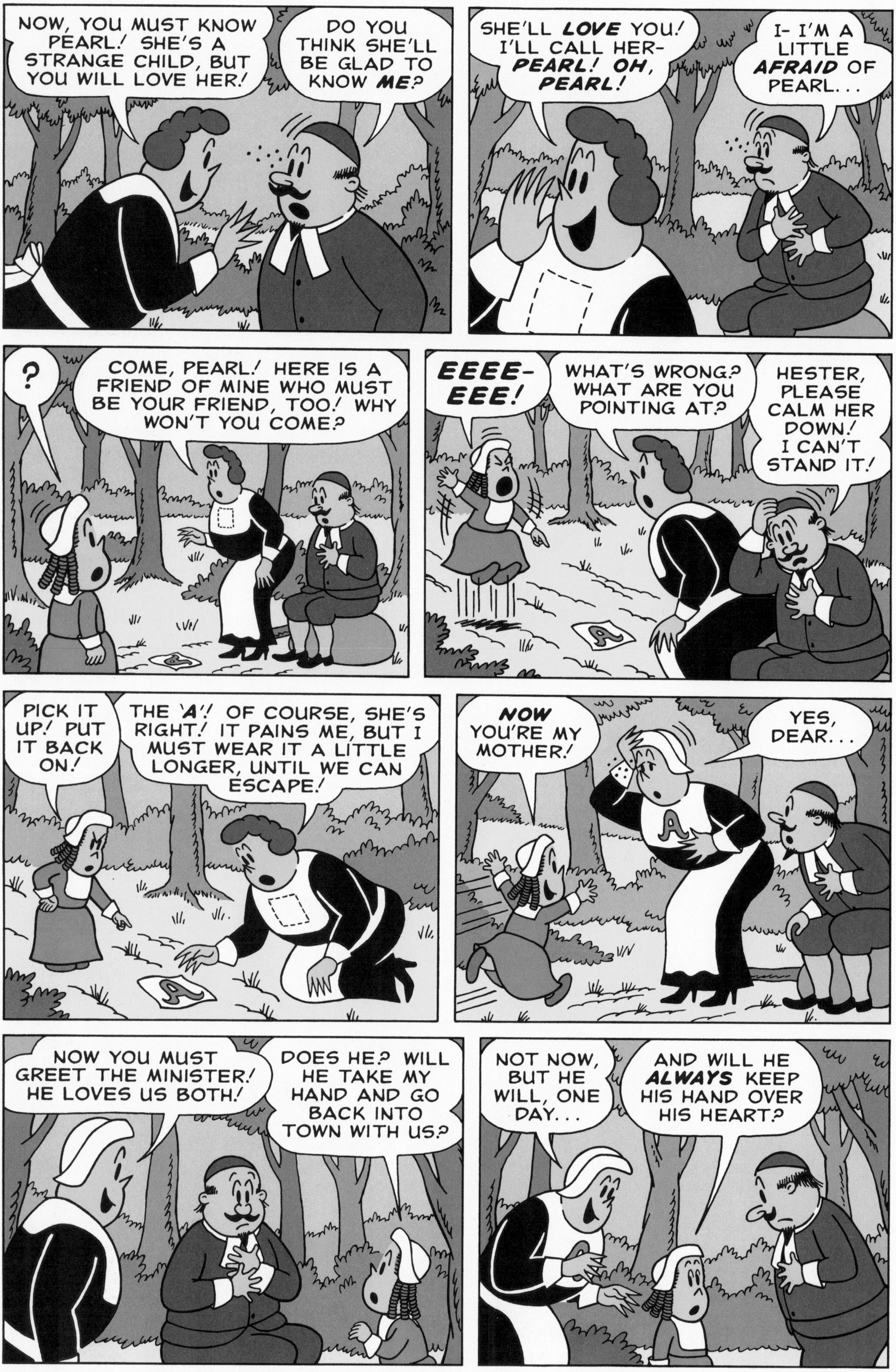
NOW, YOU MUST KNOW PEARL! SHE'S A STRANGE CHILD, BUT YOU WILL LOVE HER!
DO YOU THINK SHE'LL BE GLAD TO KNOW ME?
SHE'LL LOVE YOU! I'LL CALL HER- PEARL! OH, PEARL!
I- I'M A LITTLE AFRAID OF PEARL...
?
COME, PEARL! HERE IS A FRIEND OF MINE WHO MUST BE YOUR FRIEND, TOO! WHY WON'T YOU COME?
EEEE-EEE!
WHAT'S WRONG? WHAT ARE YOU POINTING AT?
HESTER, PLEASE CALM HER DOWN! I CAN'T STAND IT!
PICK IT UP! PUT IT BACK ON!
THE 'A'! OF COURSE, SHE'S RIGHT! IT PAINS ME, BUT I MUST WEAR IT A LITTLE LONGER, UNTIL WE CAN ESCAPE!
NOW YOU'RE MY MOTHER!
YES, DEAR...
NOW YOU MUST GREET THE MINISTER! HE LOVES US BOTH!
DOES HE? WILL HE TAKE MY HAND AND GO BACK INTO TOWN WITH US?
NOT NOW, BUT HE WILL, ONE DAY...
AND WILL HE ALWAYS KEEP HIS HAND OVER HIS HEART?

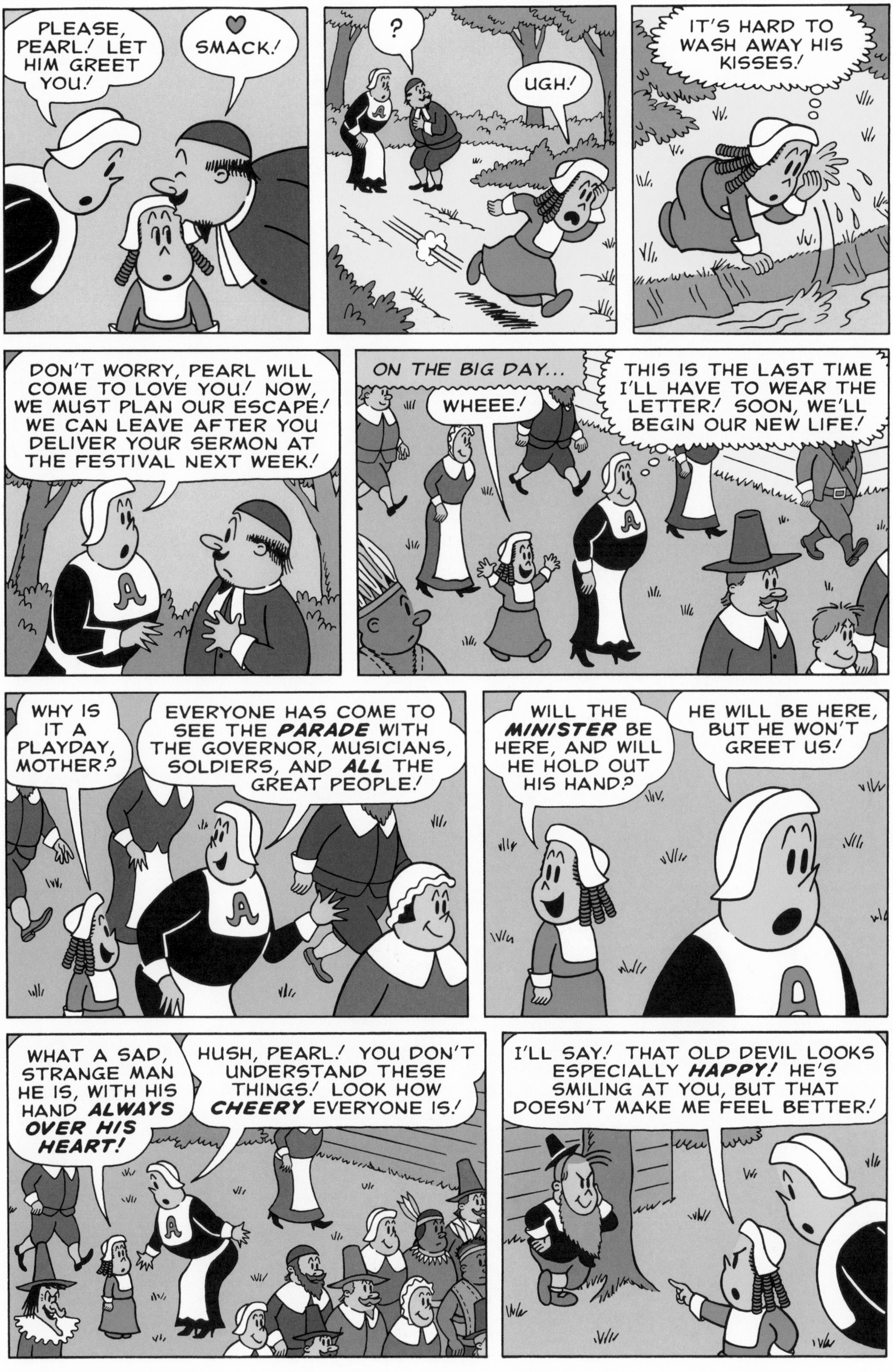

PLEASE, PEARL! LET HIM GREET YOU!
SMACK!
?
UGH!
IT'S HARD TO WASH AWAY HIS KISSES!
DON'T WORRY, PEARL WILL COME TO LOVE YOU! NOW, WE MUST PLAN OUR ESCAPE! WE CAN LEAVE AFTER YOU DELIVER YOUR SERMON AT THE FESTIVAL NEXT WEEK!
ON THE BIG DAY...
WHEEE!
THIS IS THE LAST TIME I'LL HAVE TO WEAR THE LETTER! SOON, WE'LL BEGIN OUR NEW LIFE!
WHY IS IT A PLAYDAY, MOTHER?
EVERYONE HAS COME TO SEE THE PARADE WITH THE GOVERNOR, MUSICIANS, SOLDIERS, AND ALL THE GREAT PEOPLE!
WILL THE MINISTER BE HERE, AND WILL HE HOLD OUT HIS HAND?
HE WILL BE HERE, BUT HE WON'T GREET US!
WHAT A SAD, STRANGE MAN HE IS, WITH HIS HAND ALWAYS OVER HIS HEART!
HUSH, PEARL! YOU DON'T UNDERSTAND THESE THINGS! LOOK HOW CHEERY EVERYONE IS!
I'LL SAY! THAT OLD DEVIL LOOKS ESPECIALLY HAPPY! HE'S SMILING AT YOU, BUT THAT DOESN'T MAKE ME FEEL BETTER!

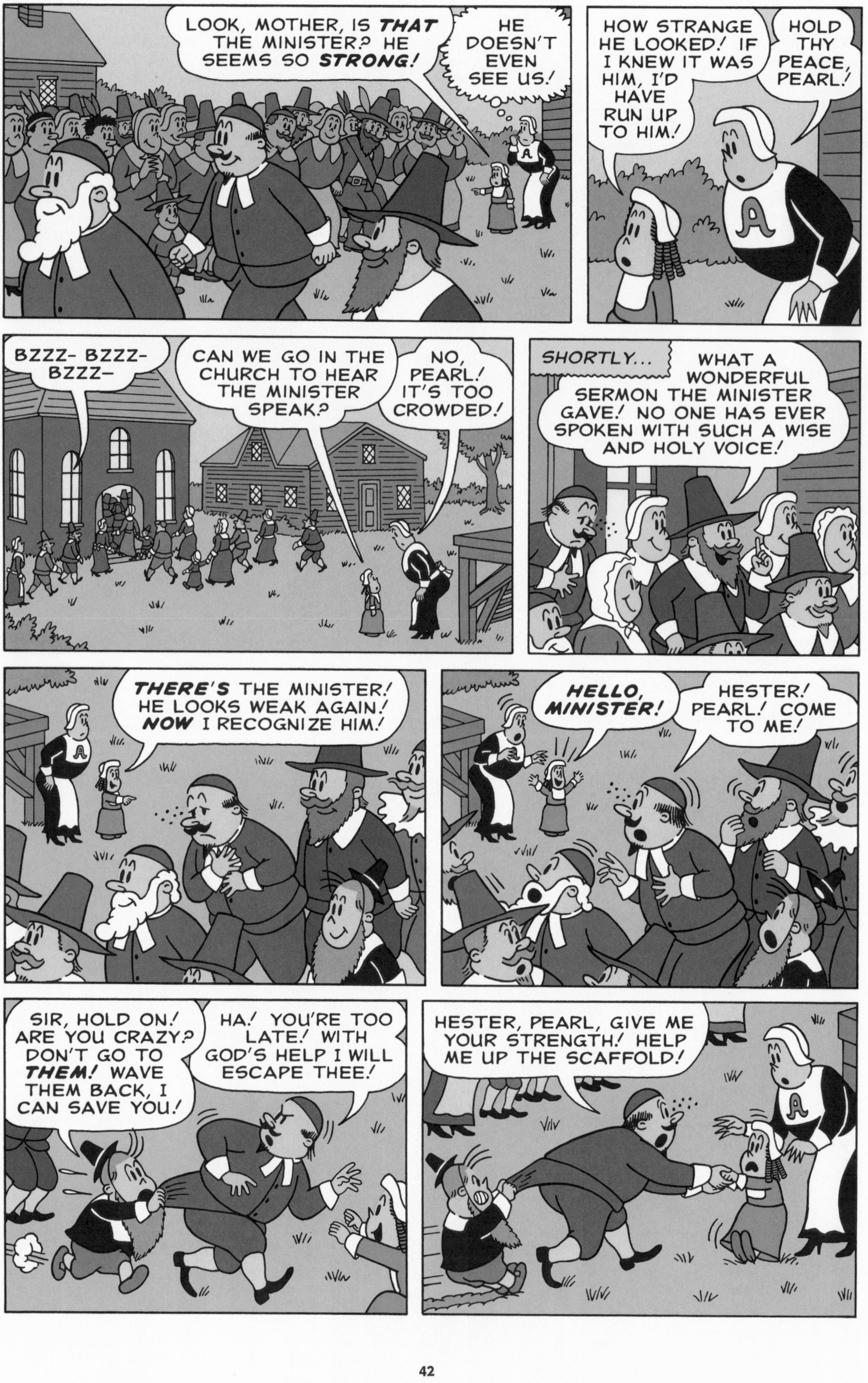
LOOK, MOTHER, IS **THAT** THE MINISTER? HE SEEMS SO **STRONG!**
HE DOESN'T EVEN SEE US!
HOW STRANGE HE LOOKED! IF I KNEW IT WAS HIM, I'D HAVE RUN UP TO HIM!
HOLD THY PEACE, PEARL!
BZZZ- BZZZ- BZZZ-
CAN WE GO IN THE CHURCH TO HEAR THE MINISTER SPEAK?
NO, PEARL! IT'S TOO CROWDED!
SHORTLY...
WHAT A WONDERFUL SERMON THE MINISTER GAVE! NO ONE HAS EVER SPOKEN WITH SUCH A WISE AND HOLY VOICE!
THERE'S THE MINISTER! HE LOOKS WEAK AGAIN! ***NOW*** I RECOGNIZE HIM!
HELLO, MINISTER!
HESTER! PEARL! COME TO ME!
SIR, HOLD ON! ARE YOU CRAZY? DON'T GO TO ***THEM!*** WAVE THEM BACK, I CAN SAVE YOU!
HA! YOU'RE TOO LATE! WITH GOD'S HELP I WILL ESCAPE THEE!
HESTER, PEARL, GIVE ME YOUR STRENGTH! HELP ME UP THE SCAFFOLD!

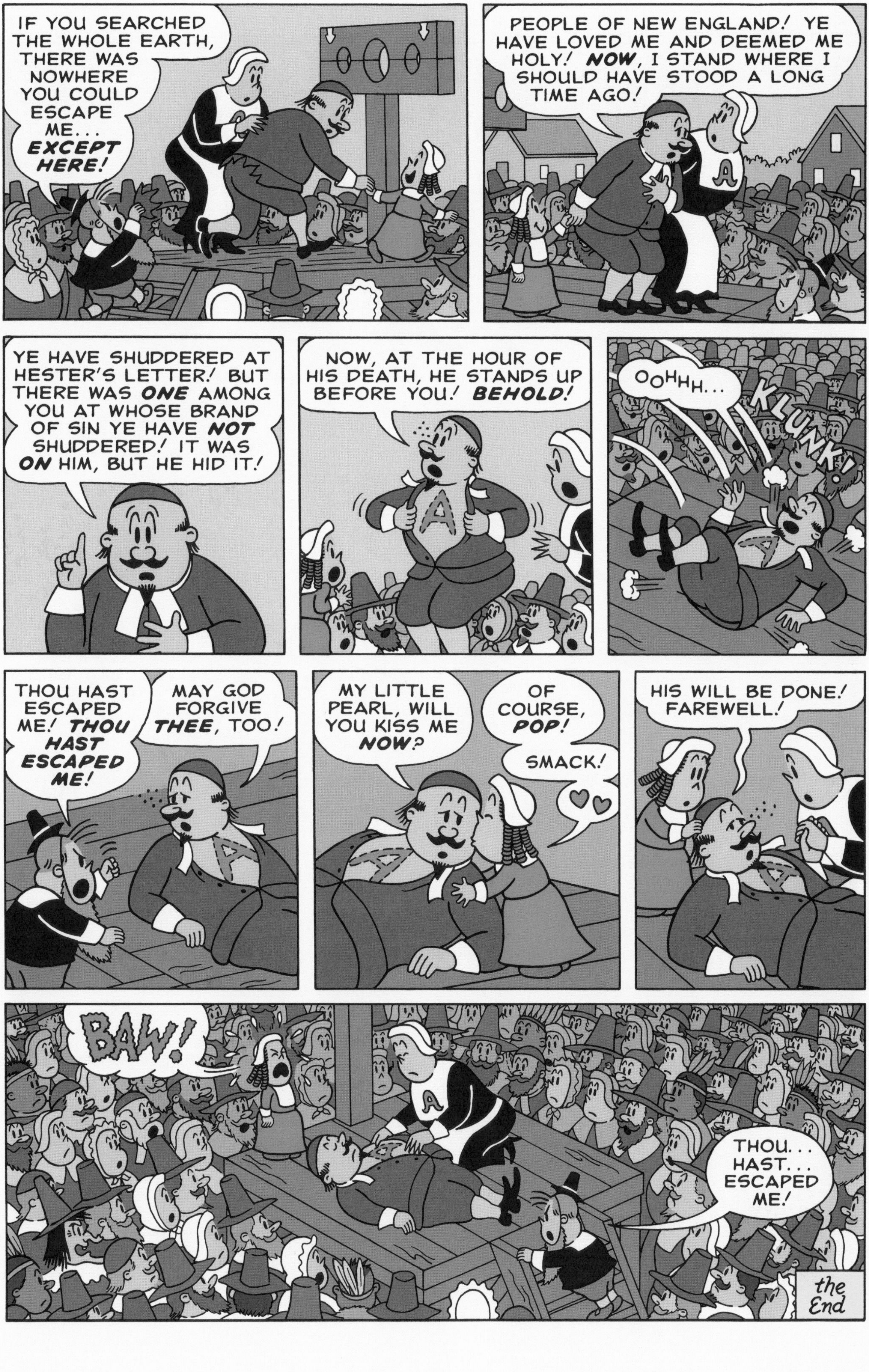
IF YOU SEARCHED THE WHOLE EARTH, THERE WAS NOWHERE YOU COULD ESCAPE ME... EXCEPT HERE!
PEOPLE OF NEW ENGLAND! YE HAVE LOVED ME AND DEEMED ME HOLY! NOW, I STAND WHERE I SHOULD HAVE STOOD A LONG TIME AGO!
YE HAVE SHUDDERED AT HESTER'S LETTER! BUT THERE WAS ONE AMONG YOU AT WHOSE BRAND OF SIN YE HAVE NOT SHUDDERED! IT WAS ON HIM, BUT HE HID IT!
NOW, AT THE HOUR OF HIS DEATH, HE STANDS UP BEFORE YOU! BEHOLD!
OOHHH...
KLUNK!
THOU HAST ESCAPED ME! THOU HAST ESCAPED ME!
MAY GOD FORGIVE THEE, TOO!
MY LITTLE PEARL, WILL YOU KISS ME NOW?
OF COURSE, POP!
SMACK!
HIS WILL BE DONE! FAREWELL!
BAW!
THOU... HAST... ESCAPED ME!
the End

PEQUOD WHALING SHIP

Over 7 Feet Long
Big Enough
For 2 Kids

Fires Harpoons
and Life-buoy
Only $6.98

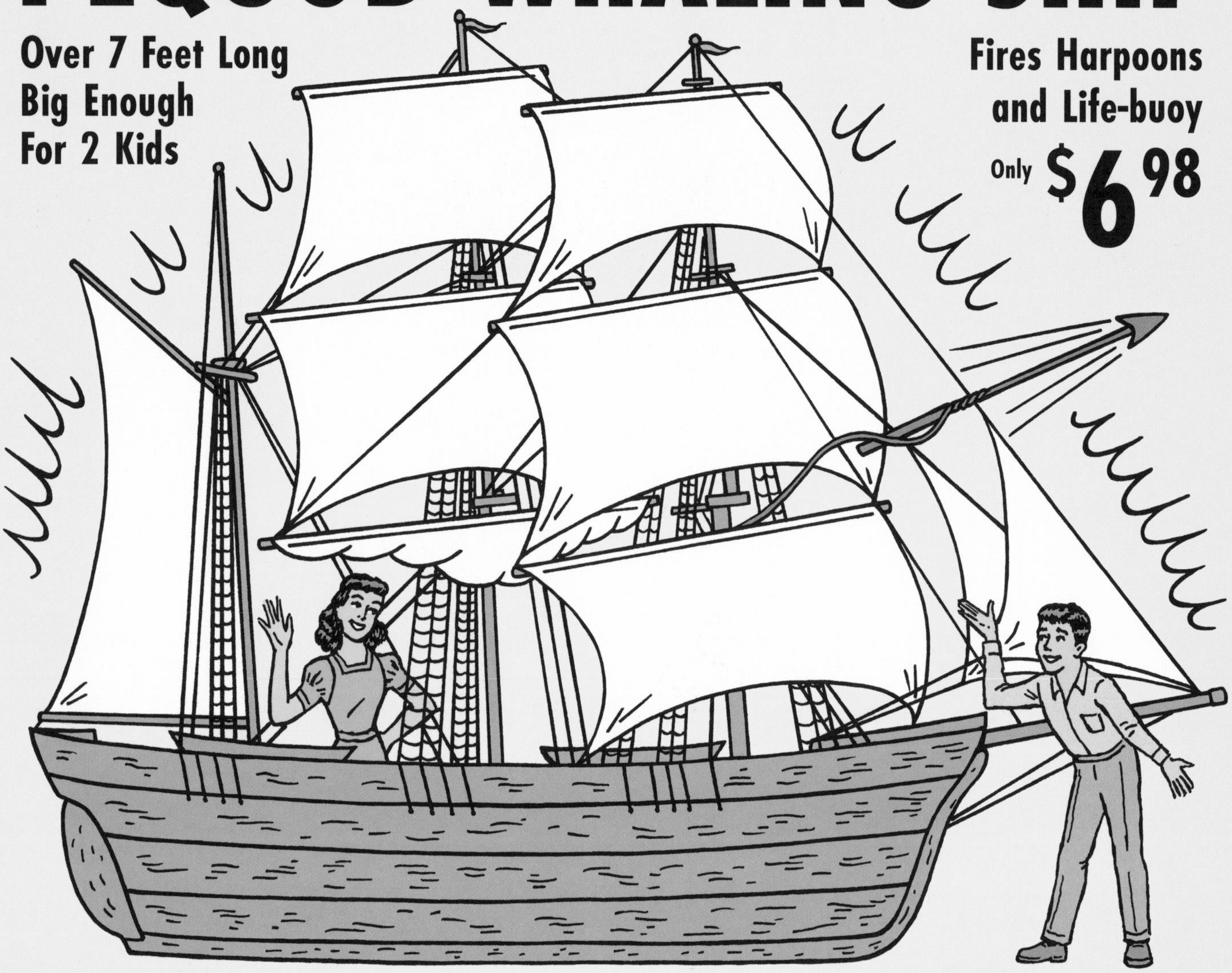

FEATURES
- Over 7 feet long
- Seats 1 kid and 1 cannibal
- Harpoons that shoot
- Harpoon lines that entangle
- Quadrant that initially works
- 3 Real masts
- 4 whale-boats
- Coffin and Life-buoy
- Sperm tubs
- Try-works
- Flame-lit forge
- Gold-plated doubloon
- Musket
- Compass needle
- and much more

How proud you will be as a crew member under Captain Ahab on your own PEQUOD WHALING SHIP – the most monomaniacal vessel in the world! What hours of imaginative play and thoughtful introspection as you and your bosom friends sail the oceans, watch from the masts, spot whales, throw harpoons, and ponder the significance of every aspect of your journey! What thrills as you play at hunting the elusive White Whale and exploring its strange and mysterious meanings! What relief when you alone escape to tell of the disaster that took the rest of the crew to the deep ocean floor!

HOURS OF ADVENTURE, YEARS OF CONTEMPLATION

Sturdily constructed of 200 lb. test fibreboard. Comes complete with ornate, beautifully written assembly instructions. Costs only $6.98 for this leviathan of fun, adventure, and single-mindedness (Because of the PEQUOD WHALING SHIP's enormous metaphorical weight we must ask for 75¢ shipping charges.)

MONEY BACK GUARANTEE

Order today and we will rush your PEQUOD WHALING SHIP to you. Use it for 3 full years. If you don't think it is the greatest ever – the most profound toy you ever had – just send it back for a full purchase price refund.

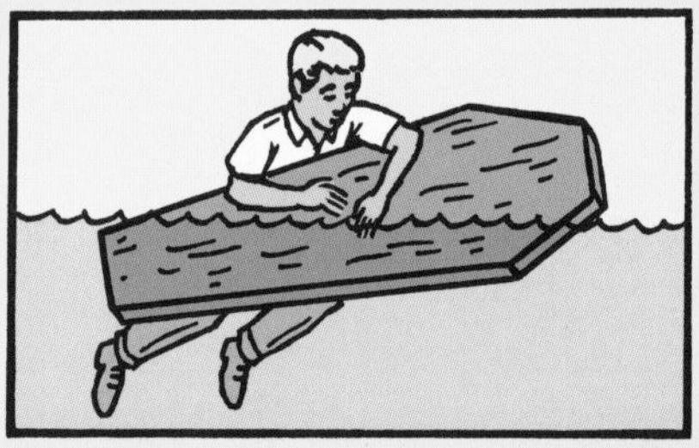

3 YEAR FREE TRIAL

HERMAN HOUSE PROD. CO. DEPT. MC1
NEW YORK, NEW YORK

Rush me my PEQUOD WHALING SHIP. I can use it for 3 years and if I am not delighted return it for full purchase price refund.

☐ SEND IT PREPAID. I enclose $6.98 plus 75¢ to help cover shipping charges.

☐ SEND IT C.O.D. I enclose $1 good-will deposit and I will pay postman $5.98 on delivery plus C.O.D. postage.

NAME____________________
ADDRESS____________________
CITY________ ZONE________ STATE________

N.Y. State residents please add 14¢ whaling tax.

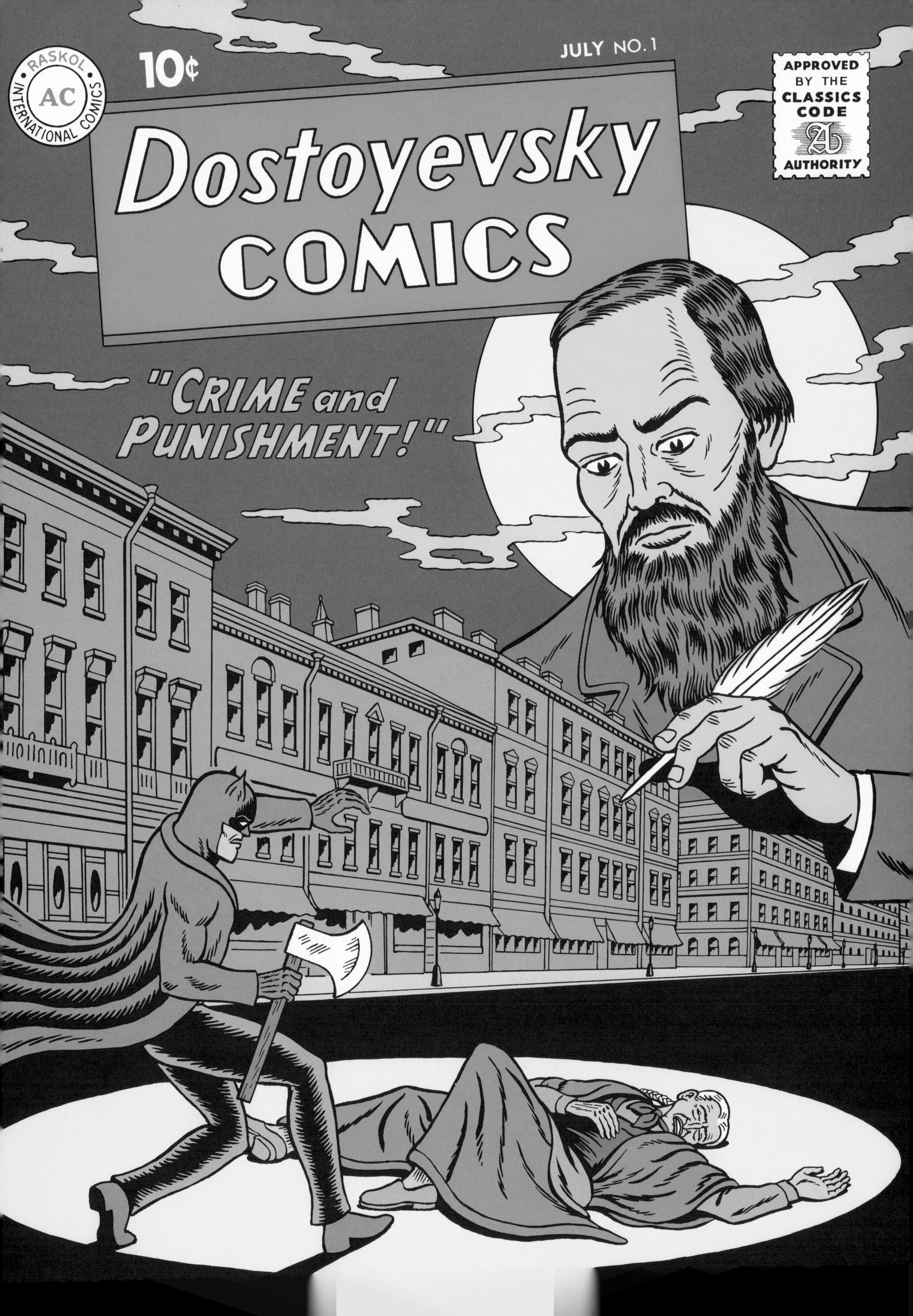
RASKOL INTERNATIONAL COMICS
AC
10¢
JULY NO. 1
APPROVED BY THE CLASSICS CODE AUTHORITY
Dostoyevsky COMICS
"CRIME and PUNISHMENT!"

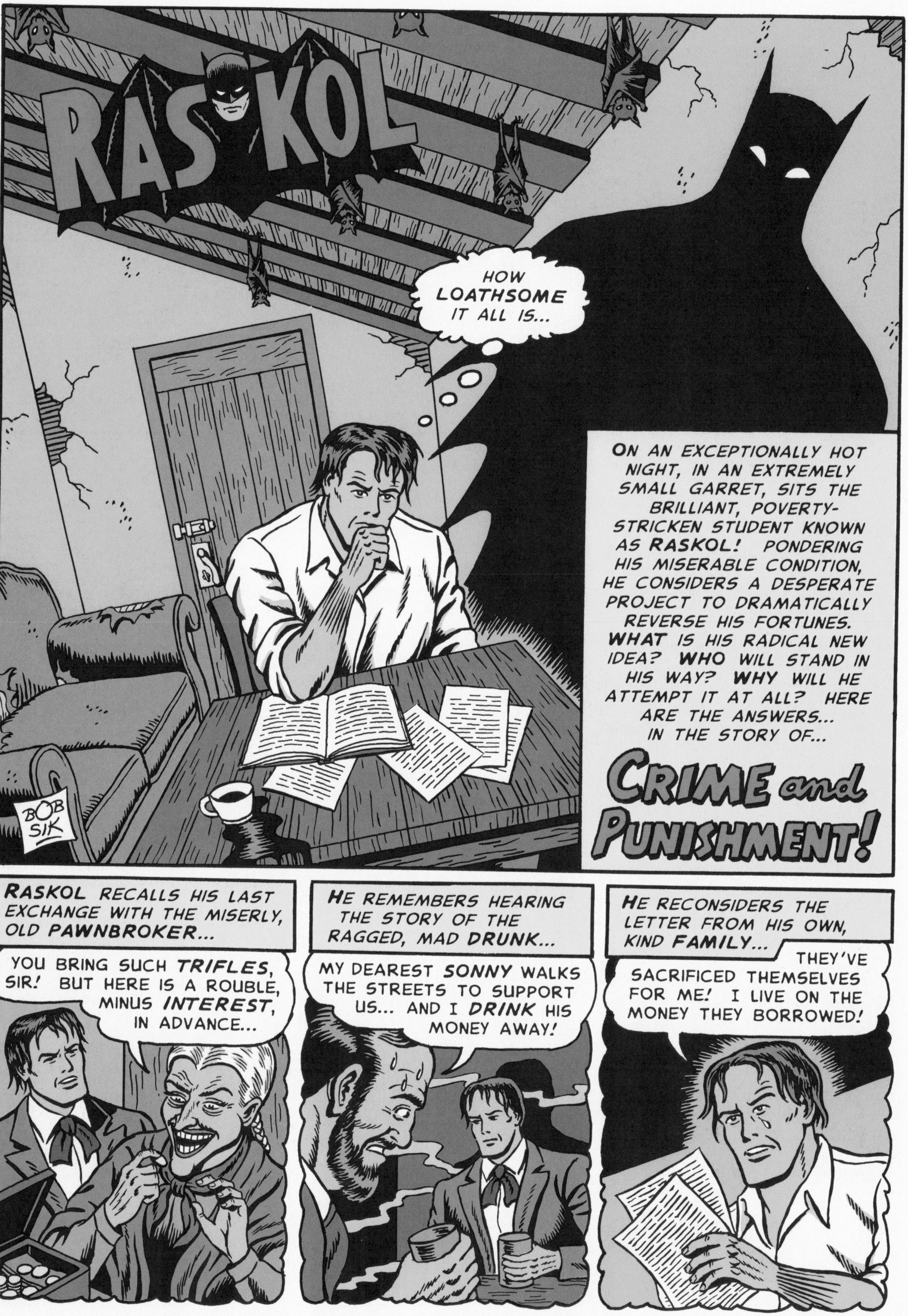
RASKOL
HOW LOATHSOME IT ALL IS...
ON AN EXCEPTIONALLY HOT NIGHT, IN AN EXTREMELY SMALL GARRET, SITS THE BRILLIANT, POVERTY-STRICKEN STUDENT KNOWN AS RASKOL! PONDERING HIS MISERABLE CONDITION, HE CONSIDERS A DESPERATE PROJECT TO DRAMATICALLY REVERSE HIS FORTUNES. WHAT IS HIS RADICAL NEW IDEA? WHO WILL STAND IN HIS WAY? WHY WILL HE ATTEMPT IT AT ALL? HERE ARE THE ANSWERS... IN THE STORY OF...
CRIME and PUNISHMENT!
BOB SIK
RASKOL RECALLS HIS LAST EXCHANGE WITH THE MISERLY, OLD PAWNBROKER...
YOU BRING SUCH TRIFLES, SIR! BUT HERE IS A ROUBLE, MINUS INTEREST, IN ADVANCE...
HE REMEMBERS HEARING THE STORY OF THE RAGGED, MAD DRUNK...
MY DEAREST SONNY WALKS THE STREETS TO SUPPORT US... AND I DRINK HIS MONEY AWAY!
HE RECONSIDERS THE LETTER FROM HIS OWN, KIND FAMILY...
THEY'VE SACRIFICED THEMSELVES FOR ME! I LIVE ON THE MONEY THEY BORROWED!

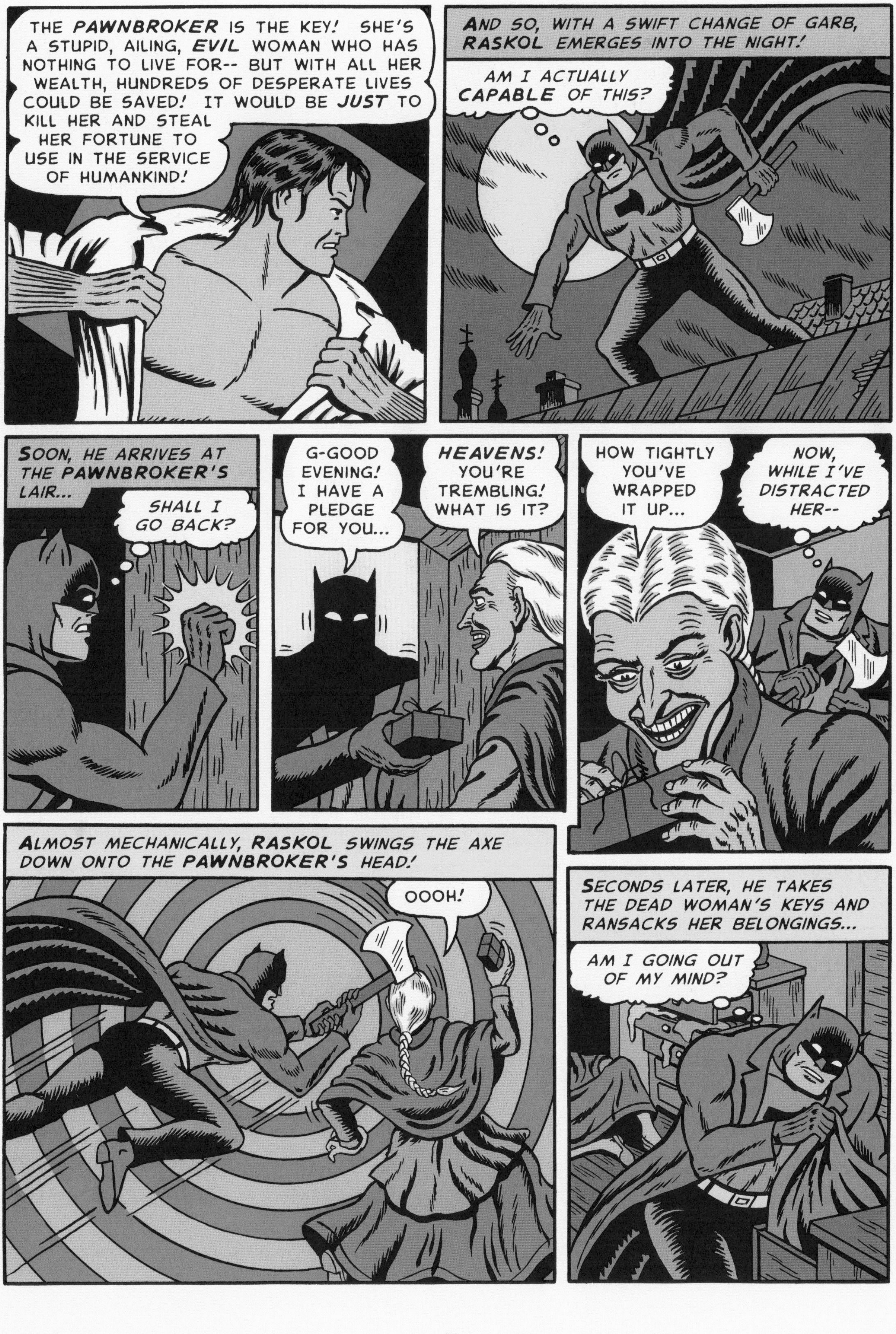
THE PAWNBROKER IS THE KEY! SHE'S A STUPID, AILING, EVIL WOMAN WHO HAS NOTHING TO LIVE FOR-- BUT WITH ALL HER WEALTH, HUNDREDS OF DESPERATE LIVES COULD BE SAVED! IT WOULD BE JUST TO KILL HER AND STEAL HER FORTUNE TO USE IN THE SERVICE OF HUMANKIND!
AND SO, WITH A SWIFT CHANGE OF GARB, RASKOL EMERGES INTO THE NIGHT!
AM I ACTUALLY CAPABLE OF THIS?
SOON, HE ARRIVES AT THE PAWNBROKER'S LAIR...
SHALL I GO BACK?
G-GOOD EVENING! I HAVE A PLEDGE FOR YOU...
HEAVENS! YOU'RE TREMBLING! WHAT IS IT?
HOW TIGHTLY YOU'VE WRAPPED IT UP...
NOW, WHILE I'VE DISTRACTED HER--
ALMOST MECHANICALLY, RASKOL SWINGS THE AXE DOWN ONTO THE PAWNBROKER'S HEAD!
OOOH!
SECONDS LATER, HE TAKES THE DEAD WOMAN'S KEYS AND RANSACKS HER BELONGINGS...
AM I GOING OUT OF MY MIND?

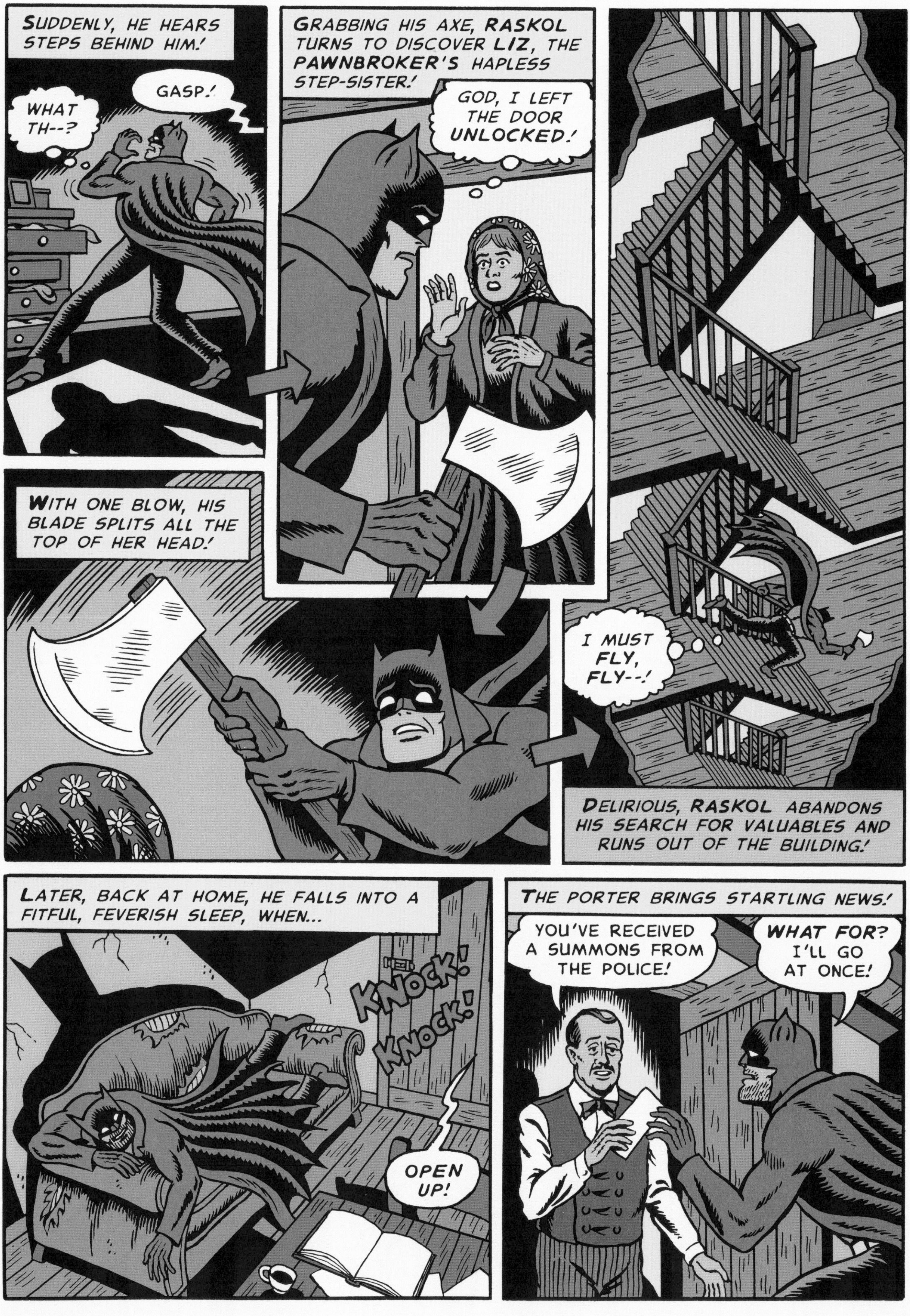
SUDDENLY, HE HEARS STEPS BEHIND HIM!
GASP!
WHAT TH--?
GRABBING HIS AXE, RASKOL TURNS TO DISCOVER LIZ, THE PAWNBROKER'S HAPLESS STEP-SISTER!
GOD, I LEFT THE DOOR UNLOCKED!
WITH ONE BLOW, HIS BLADE SPLITS ALL THE TOP OF HER HEAD!
I MUST FLY, FLY--!
DELIRIOUS, RASKOL ABANDONS HIS SEARCH FOR VALUABLES AND RUNS OUT OF THE BUILDING!
LATER, BACK AT HOME, HE FALLS INTO A FITFUL, FEVERISH SLEEP, WHEN...
KNOCK! KNOCK!
OPEN UP!
THE PORTER BRINGS STARTLING NEWS!
YOU'VE RECEIVED A SUMMONS FROM THE POLICE!
WHAT FOR? I'LL GO AT ONCE!

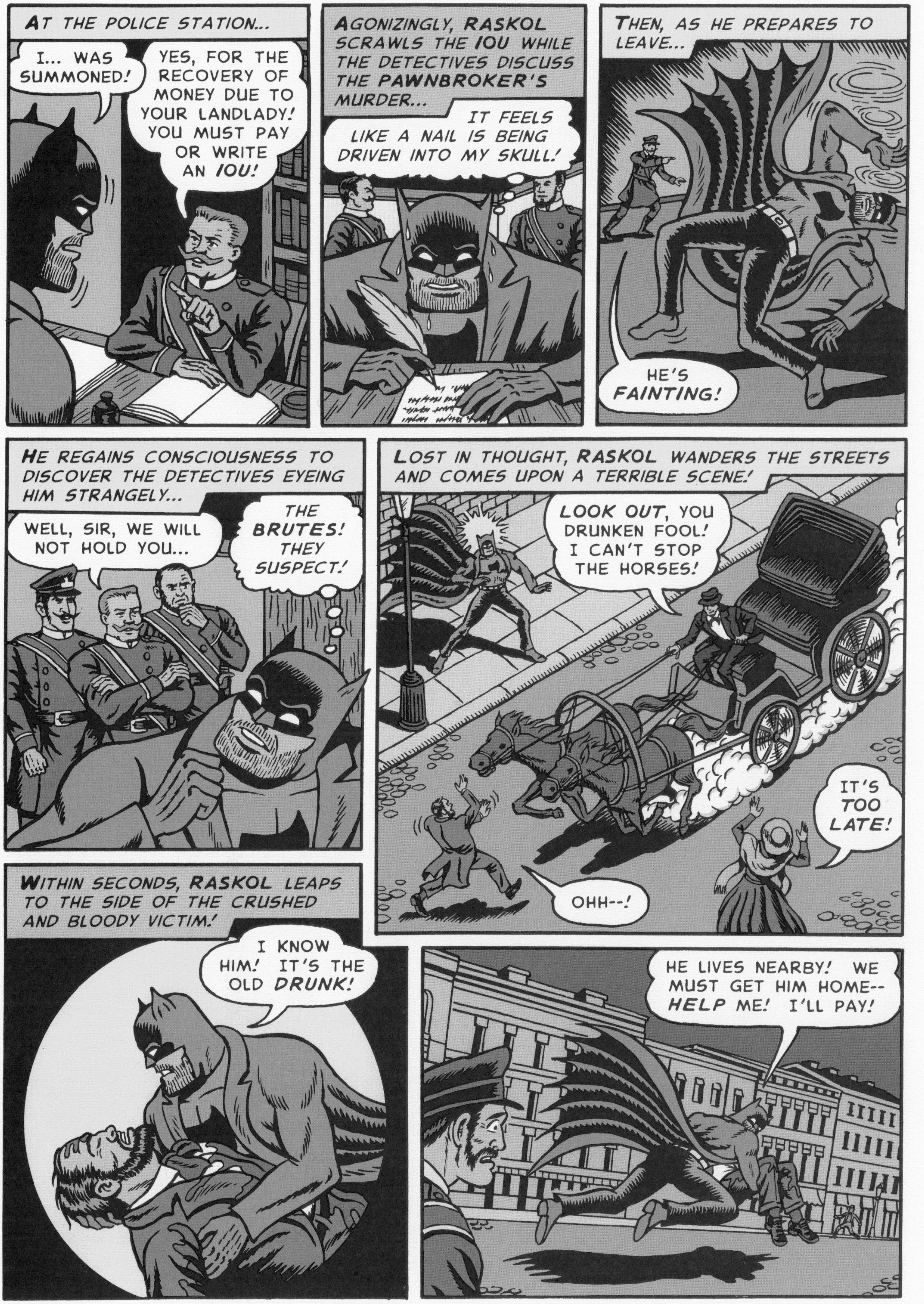
AT THE POLICE STATION...
I... WAS SUMMONED!
YES, FOR THE RECOVERY OF MONEY DUE TO YOUR LANDLADY! YOU MUST PAY OR WRITE AN IOU!
AGONIZINGLY, RASKOL SCRAWLS THE IOU WHILE THE DETECTIVES DISCUSS THE PAWNBROKER'S MURDER...
IT FEELS LIKE A NAIL IS BEING DRIVEN INTO MY SKULL!
THEN, AS HE PREPARES TO LEAVE...
HE'S FAINTING!
HE REGAINS CONSCIOUSNESS TO DISCOVER THE DETECTIVES EYEING HIM STRANGELY...
WELL, SIR, WE WILL NOT HOLD YOU...
THE BRUTES! THEY SUSPECT!
LOST IN THOUGHT, RASKOL WANDERS THE STREETS AND COMES UPON A TERRIBLE SCENE!
LOOK OUT, YOU DRUNKEN FOOL! I CAN'T STOP THE HORSES!
IT'S TOO LATE!
OHH--!
WITHIN SECONDS, RASKOL LEAPS TO THE SIDE OF THE CRUSHED AND BLOODY VICTIM!
I KNOW HIM! IT'S THE OLD DRUNK!
HE LIVES NEARBY! WE MUST GET HIM HOME-- HELP ME! I'LL PAY!

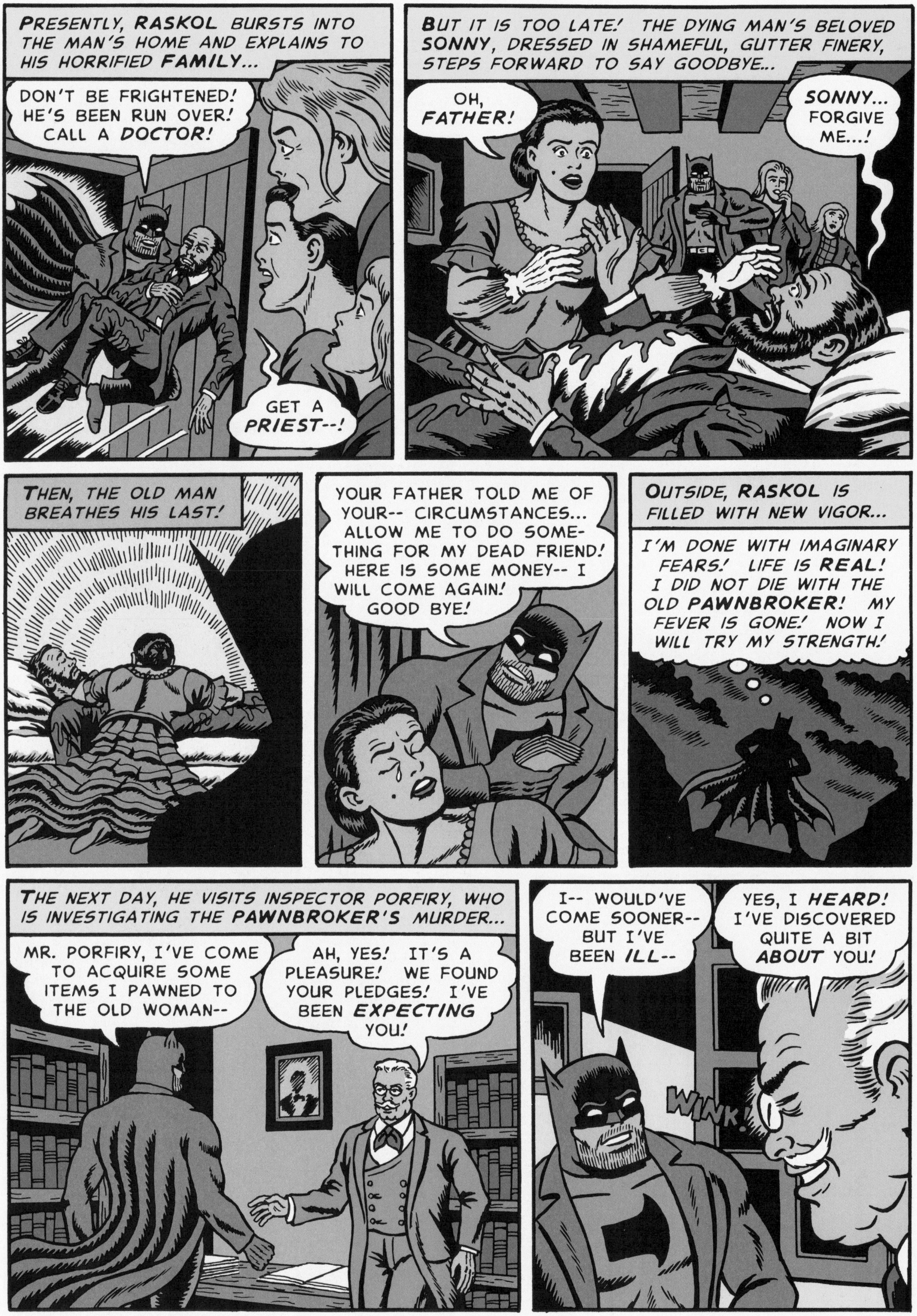
PRESENTLY, RASKOL BURSTS INTO THE MAN'S HOME AND EXPLAINS TO HIS HORRIFIED FAMILY...
DON'T BE FRIGHTENED! HE'S BEEN RUN OVER! CALL A DOCTOR!
GET A PRIEST--!
BUT IT IS TOO LATE! THE DYING MAN'S BELOVED SONNY, DRESSED IN SHAMEFUL, GUTTER FINERY, STEPS FORWARD TO SAY GOODBYE...
OH, FATHER!
SONNY... FORGIVE ME...!
THEN, THE OLD MAN BREATHES HIS LAST!
YOUR FATHER TOLD ME OF YOUR-- CIRCUMSTANCES... ALLOW ME TO DO SOMETHING FOR MY DEAD FRIEND! HERE IS SOME MONEY-- I WILL COME AGAIN! GOOD BYE!
OUTSIDE, RASKOL IS FILLED WITH NEW VIGOR...
I'M DONE WITH IMAGINARY FEARS! LIFE IS REAL! I DID NOT DIE WITH THE OLD PAWNBROKER! MY FEVER IS GONE! NOW I WILL TRY MY STRENGTH!
THE NEXT DAY, HE VISITS INSPECTOR PORFIRY, WHO IS INVESTIGATING THE PAWNBROKER'S MURDER...
MR. PORFIRY, I'VE COME TO ACQUIRE SOME ITEMS I PAWNED TO THE OLD WOMAN--
AH, YES! IT'S A PLEASURE! WE FOUND YOUR PLEDGES! I'VE BEEN EXPECTING YOU!
I-- WOULD'VE COME SOONER-- BUT I'VE BEEN ILL--
YES, I HEARD! I'VE DISCOVERED QUITE A BIT ABOUT YOU!
WINK!

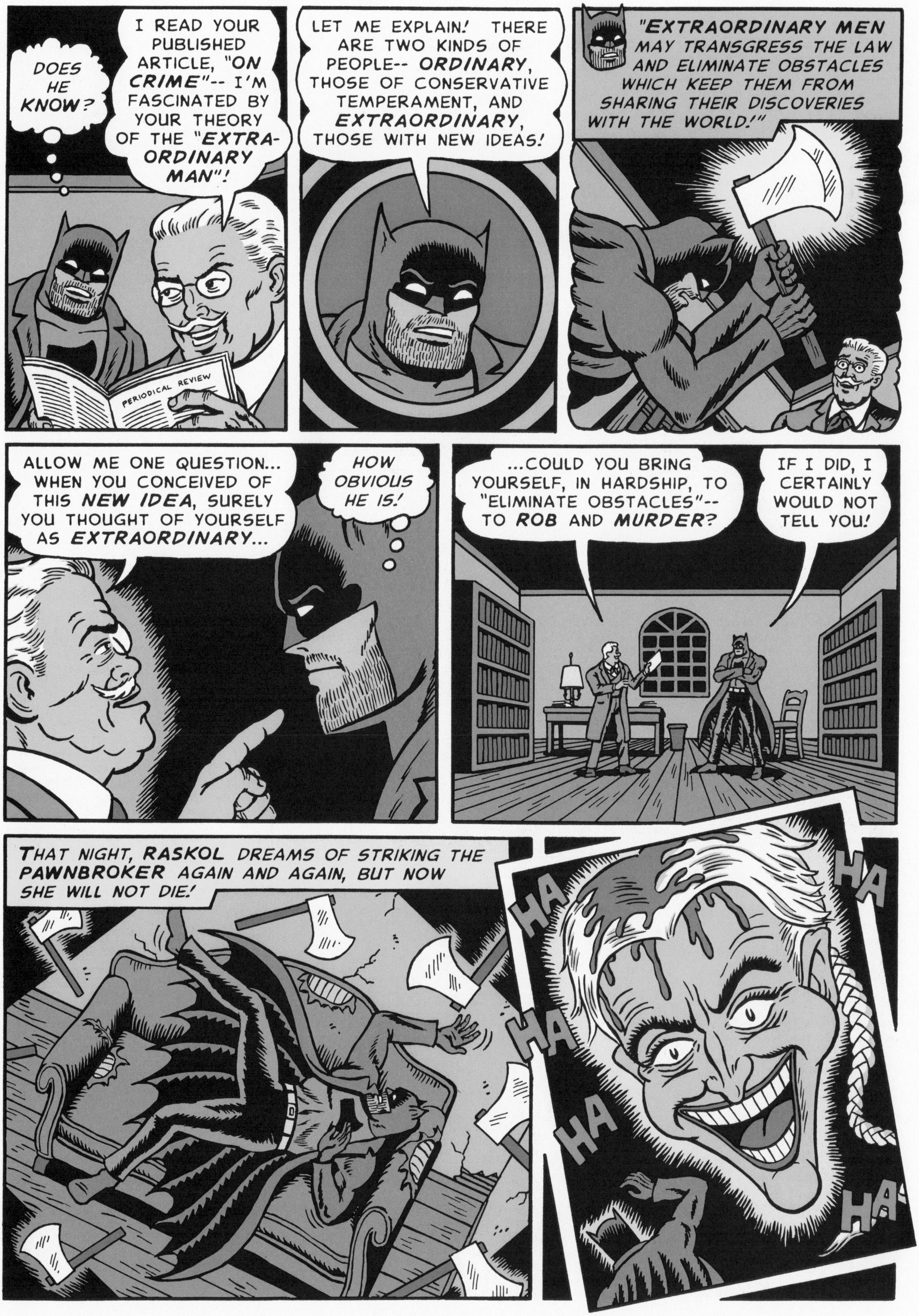

DOES HE KNOW?
I READ YOUR PUBLISHED ARTICLE, "ON CRIME"-- I'M FASCINATED BY YOUR THEORY OF THE "EXTRA-ORDINARY MAN"!
PERIODICAL REVIEW
LET ME EXPLAIN! THERE ARE TWO KINDS OF PEOPLE-- ORDINARY, THOSE OF CONSERVATIVE TEMPERAMENT, AND EXTRAORDINARY, THOSE WITH NEW IDEAS!
"EXTRAORDINARY MEN MAY TRANSGRESS THE LAW AND ELIMINATE OBSTACLES WHICH KEEP THEM FROM SHARING THEIR DISCOVERIES WITH THE WORLD!"
ALLOW ME ONE QUESTION... WHEN YOU CONCEIVED OF THIS NEW IDEA, SURELY YOU THOUGHT OF YOURSELF AS EXTRAORDINARY...
HOW OBVIOUS HE IS!
...COULD YOU BRING YOURSELF, IN HARDSHIP, TO "ELIMINATE OBSTACLES"-- TO ROB AND MURDER?
IF I DID, I CERTAINLY WOULD NOT TELL YOU!
THAT NIGHT, RASKOL DREAMS OF STRIKING THE PAWNBROKER AGAIN AND AGAIN, BUT NOW SHE WILL NOT DIE!
HA
HA
HA
HA
HA
HA

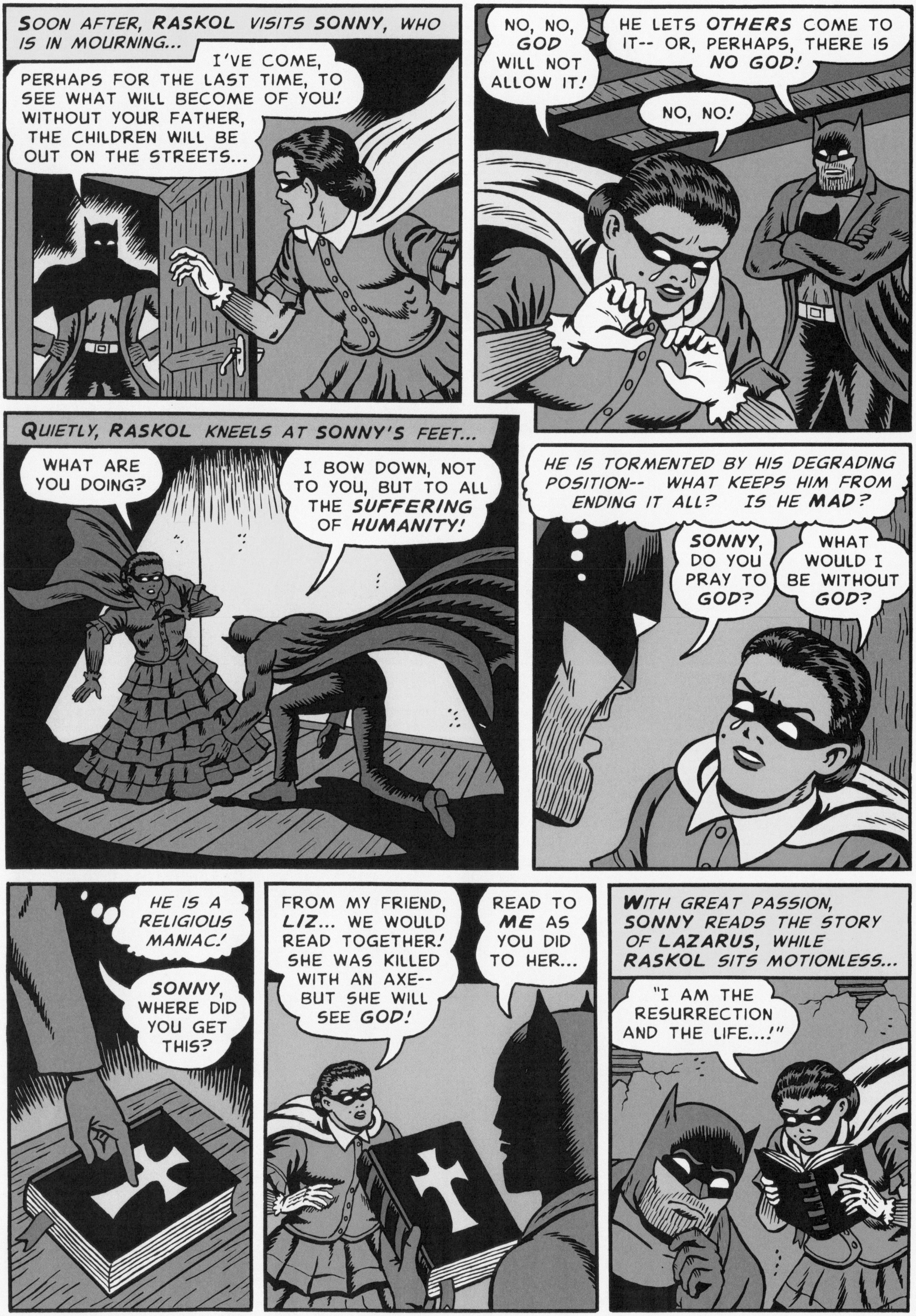
SOON AFTER, RASKOL VISITS SONNY, WHO IS IN MOURNING...
I'VE COME, PERHAPS FOR THE LAST TIME, TO SEE WHAT WILL BECOME OF YOU! WITHOUT YOUR FATHER, THE CHILDREN WILL BE OUT ON THE STREETS...
NO, NO, GOD WILL NOT ALLOW IT!
HE LETS OTHERS COME TO IT-- OR, PERHAPS, THERE IS NO GOD!
NO, NO!
QUIETLY, RASKOL KNEELS AT SONNY'S FEET...
WHAT ARE YOU DOING?
I BOW DOWN, NOT TO YOU, BUT TO ALL THE SUFFERING OF HUMANITY!
HE IS TORMENTED BY HIS DEGRADING POSITION-- WHAT KEEPS HIM FROM ENDING IT ALL? IS HE MAD?
SONNY, DO YOU PRAY TO GOD?
WHAT WOULD I BE WITHOUT GOD?
HE IS A RELIGIOUS MANIAC!
SONNY, WHERE DID YOU GET THIS?
FROM MY FRIEND, LIZ... WE WOULD READ TOGETHER! SHE WAS KILLED WITH AN AXE-- BUT SHE WILL SEE GOD!
READ TO ME AS YOU DID TO HER...
WITH GREAT PASSION, SONNY READS THE STORY OF LAZARUS, WHILE RASKOL SITS MOTIONLESS...
"I AM THE RESURRECTION AND THE LIFE...!"

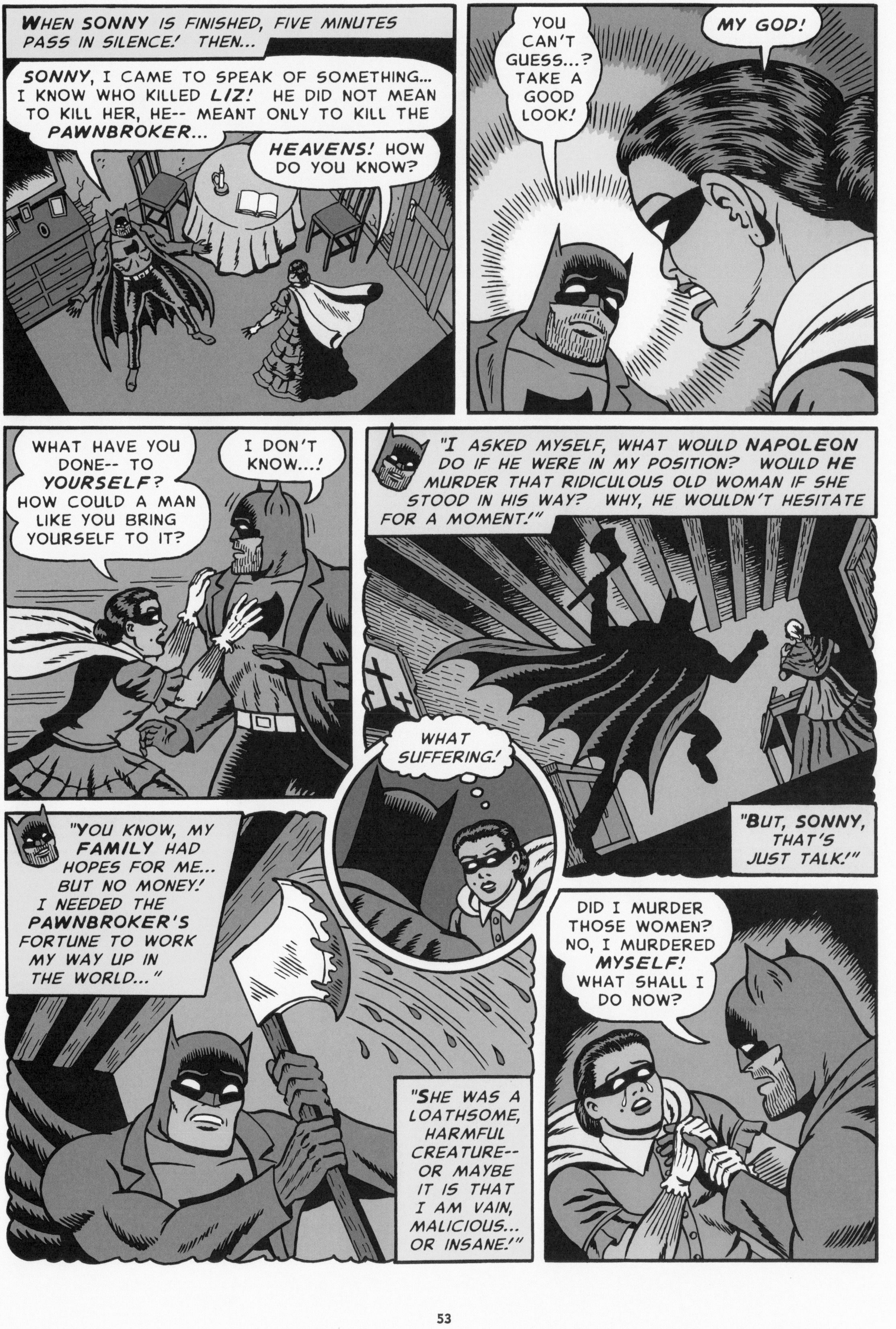
WHEN SONNY IS FINISHED, FIVE MINUTES PASS IN SILENCE! THEN...
SONNY, I CAME TO SPEAK OF SOMETHING... I KNOW WHO KILLED LIZ! HE DID NOT MEAN TO KILL HER, HE-- MEANT ONLY TO KILL THE PAWNBROKER...
HEAVENS! HOW DO YOU KNOW?
YOU CAN'T GUESS...? TAKE A GOOD LOOK!
MY GOD!
WHAT HAVE YOU DONE-- TO YOURSELF? HOW COULD A MAN LIKE YOU BRING YOURSELF TO IT?
I DON'T KNOW...!
"I ASKED MYSELF, WHAT WOULD NAPOLEON DO IF HE WERE IN MY POSITION? WOULD HE MURDER THAT RIDICULOUS OLD WOMAN IF SHE STOOD IN HIS WAY? WHY, HE WOULDN'T HESITATE FOR A MOMENT!"
WHAT SUFFERING!
"BUT, SONNY, THAT'S JUST TALK!"
"YOU KNOW, MY FAMILY HAD HOPES FOR ME... BUT NO MONEY! I NEEDED THE PAWNBROKER'S FORTUNE TO WORK MY WAY UP IN THE WORLD..."
"SHE WAS A LOATHSOME, HARMFUL CREATURE-- OR MAYBE IT IS THAT I AM VAIN, MALICIOUS... OR INSANE!"
DID I MURDER THOSE WOMEN? NO, I MURDERED MYSELF! WHAT SHALL I DO NOW?

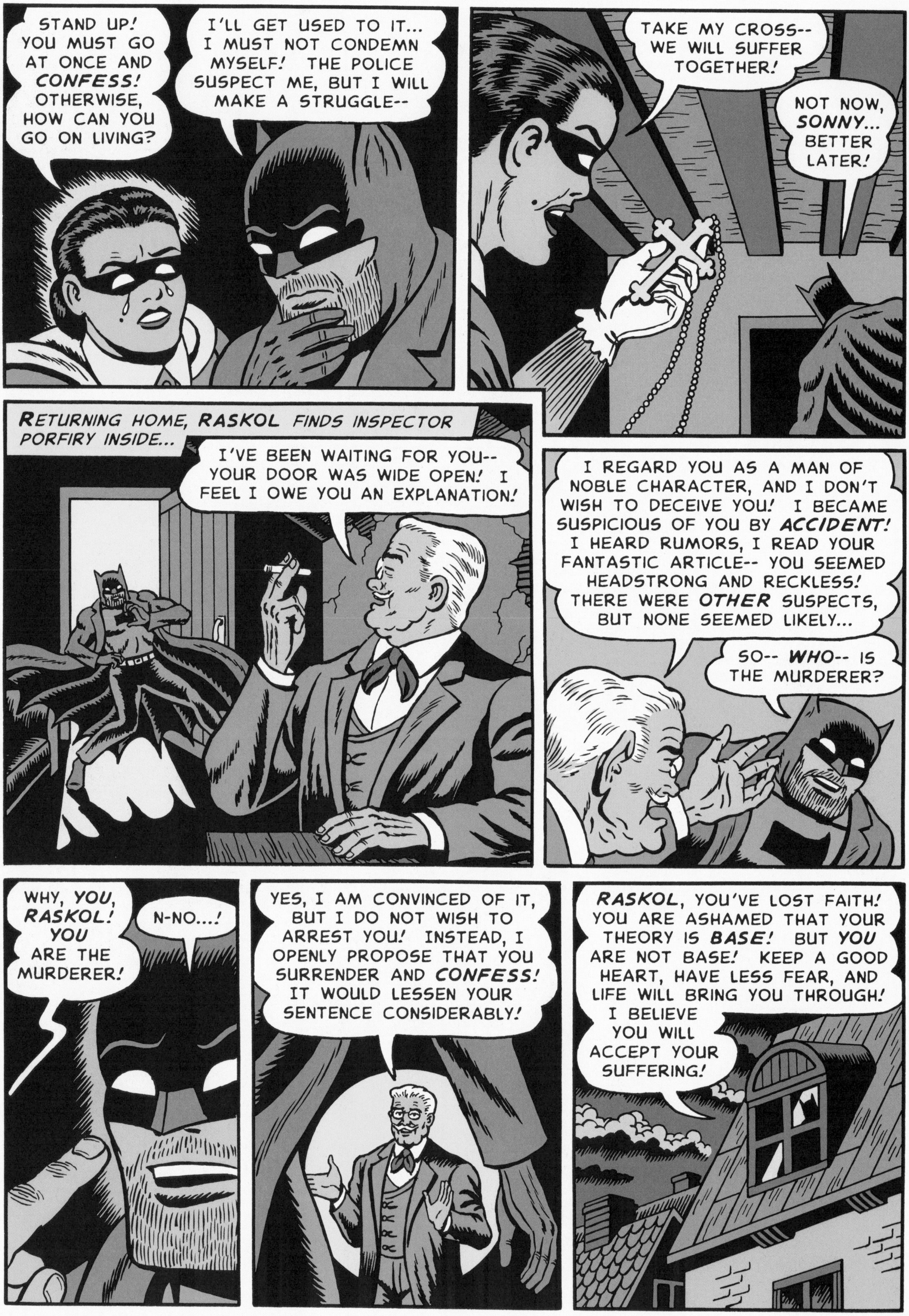
STAND UP! YOU MUST GO AT ONCE AND CONFESS! OTHERWISE, HOW CAN YOU GO ON LIVING?
I'LL GET USED TO IT... I MUST NOT CONDEMN MYSELF! THE POLICE SUSPECT ME, BUT I WILL MAKE A STRUGGLE--
TAKE MY CROSS-- WE WILL SUFFER TOGETHER!
NOT NOW, SONNY... BETTER LATER!
RETURNING HOME, RASKOL FINDS INSPECTOR PORFIRY INSIDE...
I'VE BEEN WAITING FOR YOU-- YOUR DOOR WAS WIDE OPEN! I FEEL I OWE YOU AN EXPLANATION!
I REGARD YOU AS A MAN OF NOBLE CHARACTER, AND I DON'T WISH TO DECEIVE YOU! I BECAME SUSPICIOUS OF YOU BY ACCIDENT! I HEARD RUMORS, I READ YOUR FANTASTIC ARTICLE-- YOU SEEMED HEADSTRONG AND RECKLESS! THERE WERE OTHER SUSPECTS, BUT NONE SEEMED LIKELY...
SO-- WHO-- IS THE MURDERER?
WHY, YOU, RASKOL! YOU ARE THE MURDERER!
N-NO...!
YES, I AM CONVINCED OF IT, BUT I DO NOT WISH TO ARREST YOU! INSTEAD, I OPENLY PROPOSE THAT YOU SURRENDER AND CONFESS! IT WOULD LESSEN YOUR SENTENCE CONSIDERABLY!
RASKOL, YOU'VE LOST FAITH! YOU ARE ASHAMED THAT YOUR THEORY IS BASE! BUT YOU ARE NOT BASE! KEEP A GOOD HEART, HAVE LESS FEAR, AND LIFE WILL BRING YOU THROUGH!
I BELIEVE YOU WILL ACCEPT YOUR SUFFERING!

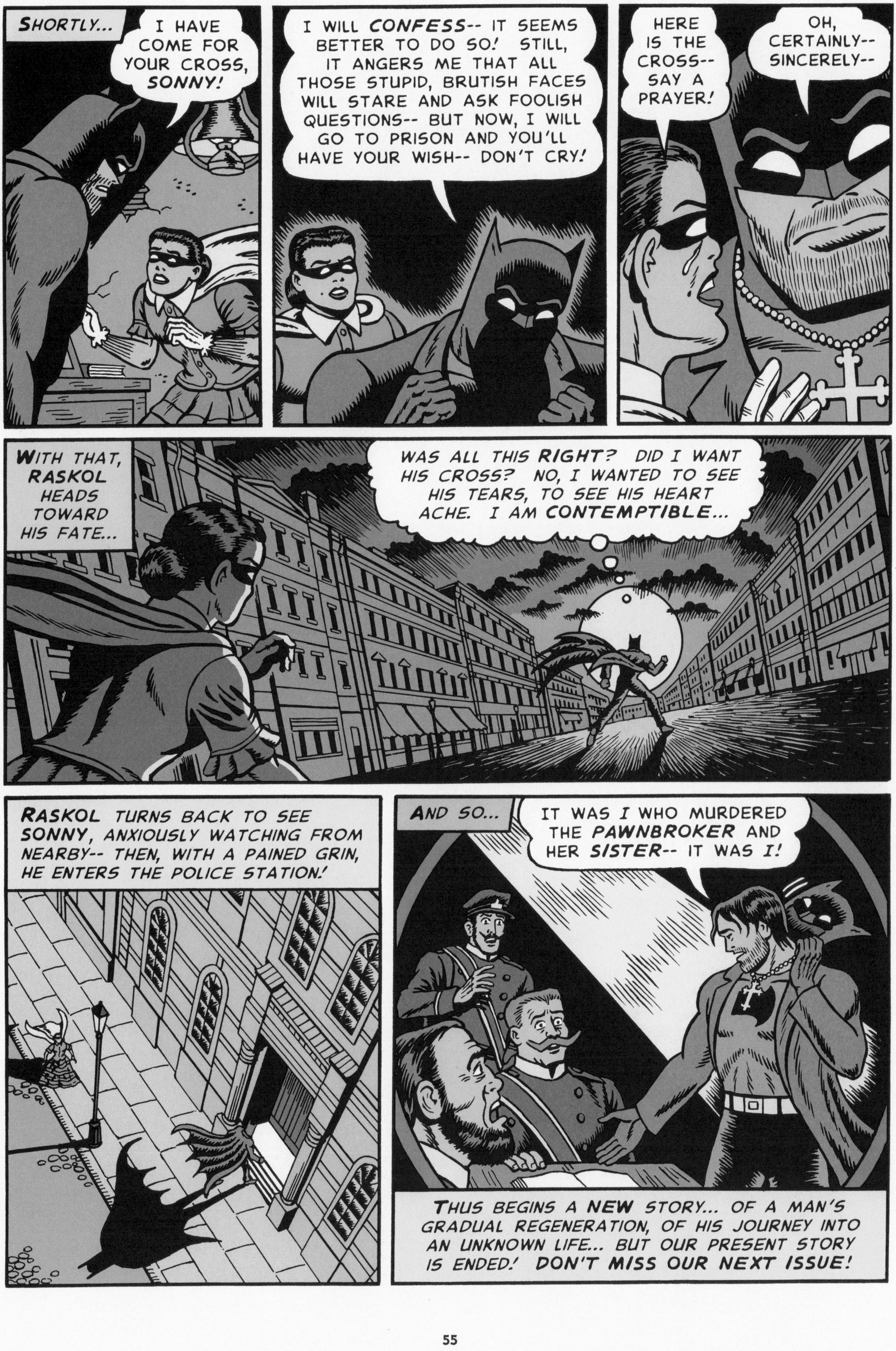
SHORTLY...
I HAVE COME FOR YOUR CROSS, SONNY!
I WILL CONFESS-- IT SEEMS BETTER TO DO SO! STILL, IT ANGERS ME THAT ALL THOSE STUPID, BRUTISH FACES WILL STARE AND ASK FOOLISH QUESTIONS-- BUT NOW, I WILL GO TO PRISON AND YOU'LL HAVE YOUR WISH-- DON'T CRY!
HERE IS THE CROSS-- SAY A PRAYER!
OH, CERTAINLY-- SINCERELY--
WITH THAT, RASKOL HEADS TOWARD HIS FATE...
WAS ALL THIS RIGHT? DID I WANT HIS CROSS? NO, I WANTED TO SEE HIS TEARS, TO SEE HIS HEART ACHE. I AM CONTEMPTIBLE...
RASKOL TURNS BACK TO SEE SONNY, ANXIOUSLY WATCHING FROM NEARBY-- THEN, WITH A PAINED GRIN, HE ENTERS THE POLICE STATION!
AND SO...
IT WAS I WHO MURDERED THE PAWNBROKER AND HER SISTER-- IT WAS I!
THUS BEGINS A NEW STORY... OF A MAN'S GRADUAL REGENERATION, OF HIS JOURNEY INTO AN UNKNOWN LIFE... BUT OUR PRESENT STORY IS ENDED! DON'T MISS OUR NEXT ISSUE!

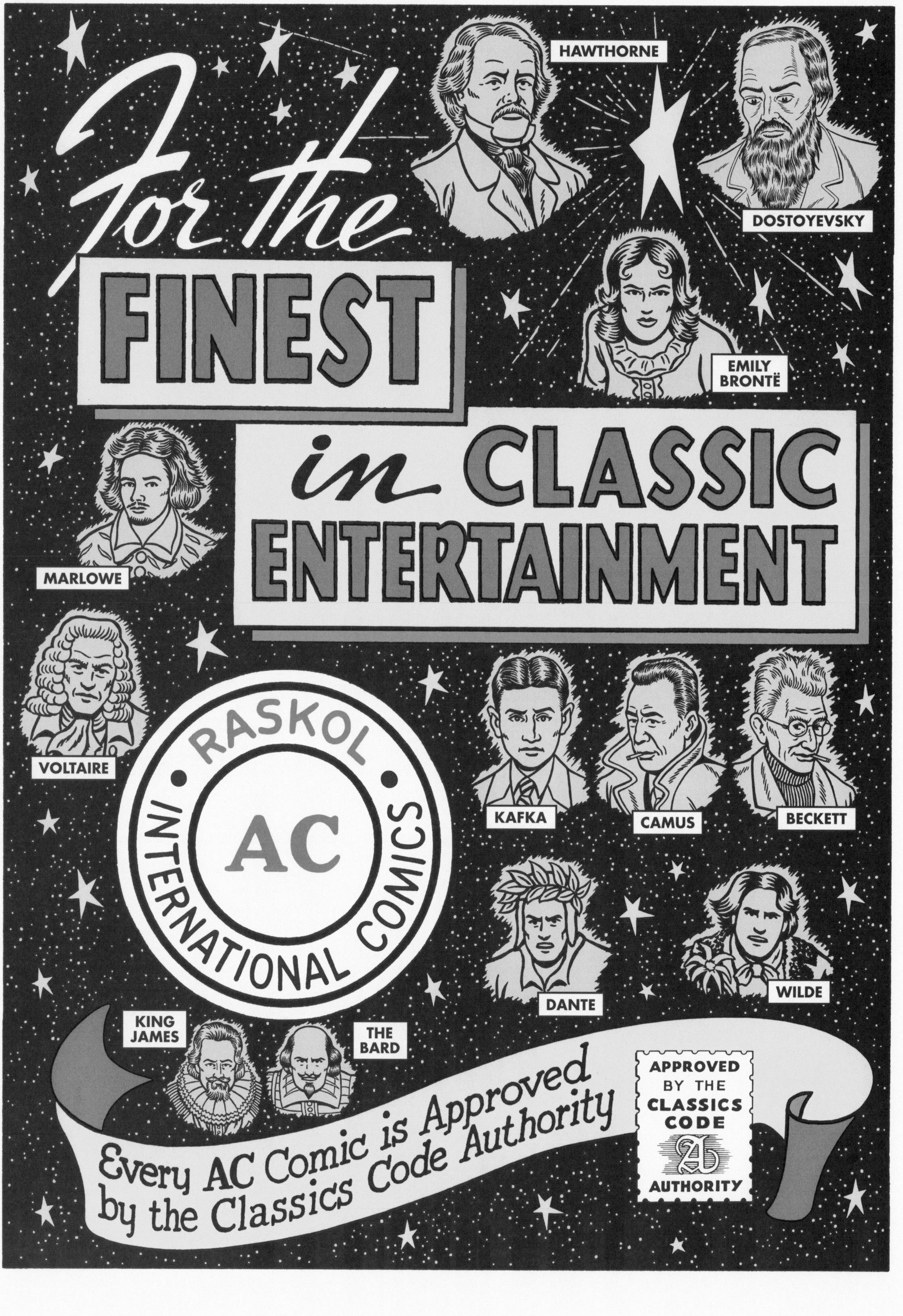
For the
FINEST
in CLASSIC
ENTERTAINMENT
HAWTHORNE
DOSTOYEVSKY
EMILY BRONTË
MARLOWE
VOLTAIRE
RASKOL
AC
INTERNATIONAL COMICS
KAFKA
CAMUS
BECKETT
DANTE
WILDE
KING JAMES
THE BARD
Every AC Comic is Approved by the Classics Code Authority
APPROVED BY THE CLASSICS CODE AUTHORITY

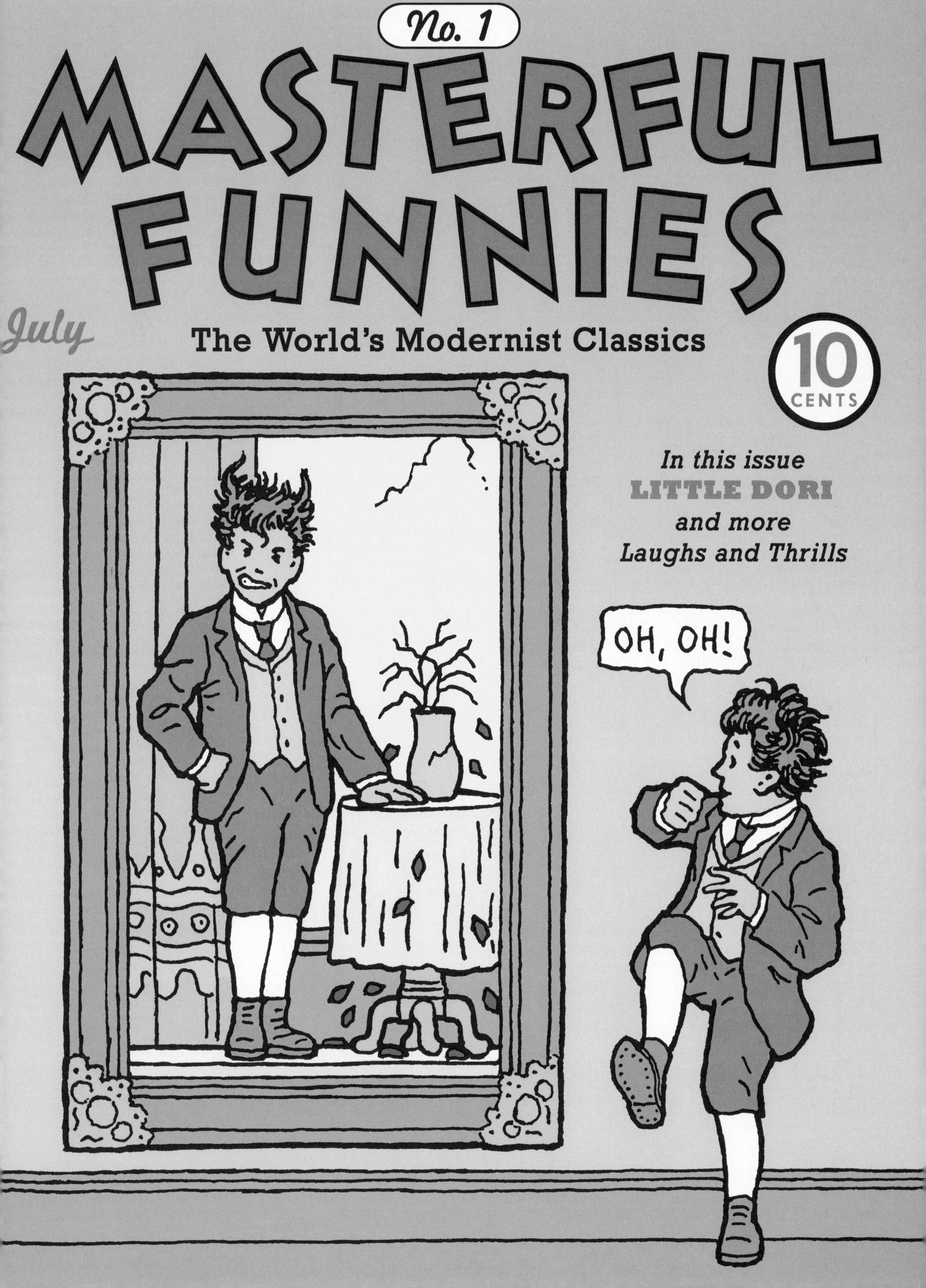
No. 1
MASTERFUL FUNNIES
July
The World's Modernist Classics
10 CENTS
In this issue
LITTLE DORI
and more
Laughs and Thrills
OH, OH!

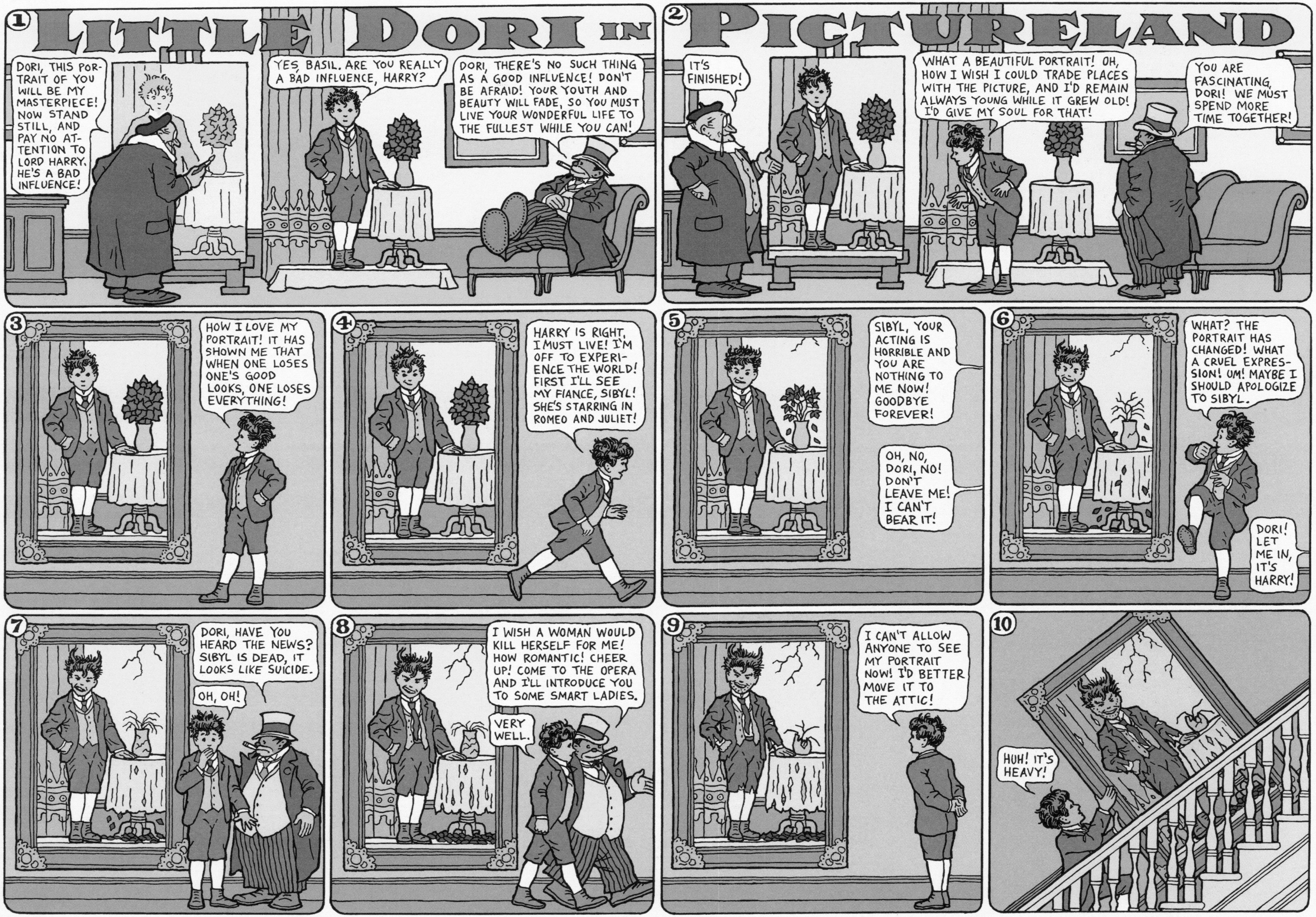
LITTLE DORI IN PICTURELAND
1
DORI, THIS PORTRAIT OF YOU WILL BE MY MASTERPIECE! NOW STAND STILL, AND PAY NO ATTENTION TO LORD HARRY. HE'S A BAD INFLUENCE!
YES, BASIL. ARE YOU REALLY A BAD INFLUENCE, HARRY?
DORI, THERE'S NO SUCH THING AS A GOOD INFLUENCE! DON'T BE AFRAID! YOUR YOUTH AND BEAUTY WILL FADE, SO YOU MUST LIVE YOUR WONDERFUL LIFE TO THE FULLEST WHILE YOU CAN!
2
IT'S FINISHED!
WHAT A BEAUTIFUL PORTRAIT! OH, HOW I WISH I COULD TRADE PLACES WITH THE PICTURE, AND I'D REMAIN ALWAYS YOUNG WHILE IT GREW OLD! I'D GIVE MY SOUL FOR THAT!
YOU ARE FASCINATING, DORI! WE MUST SPEND MORE TIME TOGETHER!
3
HOW I LOVE MY PORTRAIT! IT HAS SHOWN ME THAT WHEN ONE LOSES ONE'S GOOD LOOKS, ONE LOSES EVERYTHING!
4
HARRY IS RIGHT, I MUST LIVE! I'M OFF TO EXPERIENCE THE WORLD! FIRST I'LL SEE MY FIANCE, SIBYL! SHE'S STARRING IN ROMEO AND JULIET!
5
SIBYL, YOUR ACTING IS HORRIBLE AND YOU ARE NOTHING TO ME NOW! GOODBYE FOREVER!
OH, NO, DORI, NO! DON'T LEAVE ME! I CAN'T BEAR IT!
6
WHAT? THE PORTRAIT HAS CHANGED! WHAT A CRUEL EXPRESSION! UM! MAYBE I SHOULD APOLOGIZE TO SIBYL.
DORI! LET ME IN, IT'S HARRY!
7
DORI, HAVE YOU HEARD THE NEWS? SIBYL IS DEAD, IT LOOKS LIKE SUICIDE.
OH, OH!
8
I WISH A WOMAN WOULD KILL HERSELF FOR ME! HOW ROMANTIC! CHEER UP! COME TO THE OPERA AND I'LL INTRODUCE YOU TO SOME SMART LADIES.
VERY WELL.
9
I CAN'T ALLOW ANYONE TO SEE MY PORTRAIT NOW! I'D BETTER MOVE IT TO THE ATTIC!
10
HUH! IT'S HEAVY!

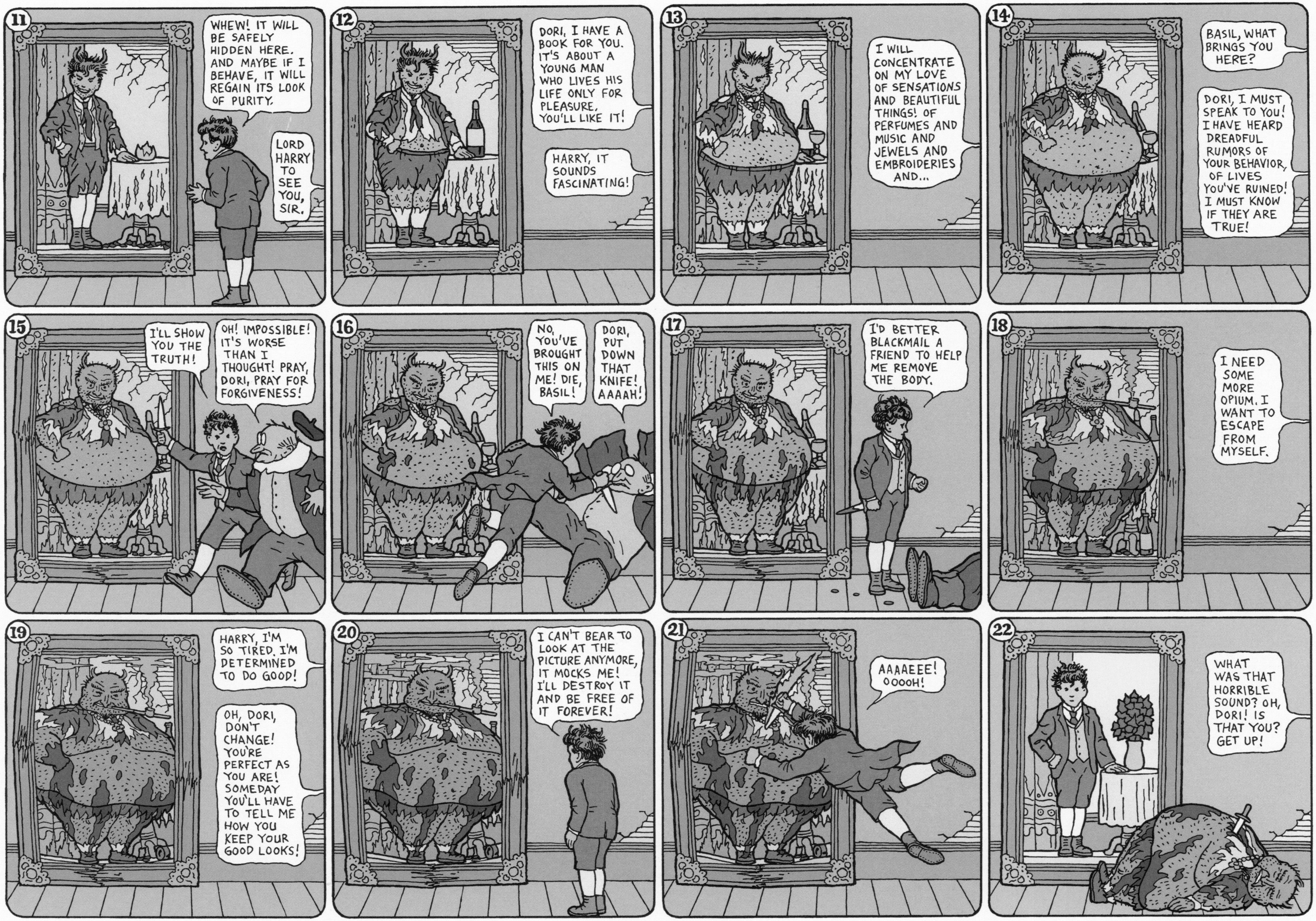
11
WHEW! IT WILL BE SAFELY HIDDEN HERE. AND MAYBE IF I BEHAVE, IT WILL REGAIN ITS LOOK OF PURITY.
LORD HARRY TO SEE YOU, SIR.
12
DORI, I HAVE A BOOK FOR YOU. IT'S ABOUT A YOUNG MAN WHO LIVES HIS LIFE ONLY FOR PLEASURE, YOU'LL LIKE IT!
HARRY, IT SOUNDS FASCINATING!
13
I WILL CONCENTRATE ON MY LOVE OF SENSATIONS AND BEAUTIFUL THINGS! OF PERFUMES AND MUSIC AND JEWELS AND EMBROIDERIES AND...
14
BASIL, WHAT BRINGS YOU HERE?
DORI, I MUST SPEAK TO YOU! I HAVE HEARD DREADFUL RUMORS OF YOUR BEHAVIOR, OF LIVES YOU'VE RUINED! I MUST KNOW IF THEY ARE TRUE!
15
I'LL SHOW YOU THE TRUTH!
OH! IMPOSSIBLE! IT'S WORSE THAN I THOUGHT! PRAY, DORI, PRAY FOR FORGIVENESS!
16
NO, YOU'VE BROUGHT THIS ON ME! DIE, BASIL!
DORI, PUT DOWN THAT KNIFE! AAAAH!
17
I'D BETTER BLACKMAIL A FRIEND TO HELP ME REMOVE THE BODY.
18
I NEED SOME MORE OPIUM. I WANT TO ESCAPE FROM MYSELF.
19
HARRY, I'M SO TIRED. I'M DETERMINED TO DO GOOD!
OH, DORI, DON'T CHANGE! YOU'RE PERFECT AS YOU ARE! SOMEDAY YOU'LL HAVE TO TELL ME HOW YOU KEEP YOUR GOOD LOOKS!
20
I CAN'T BEAR TO LOOK AT THE PICTURE ANYMORE, IT MOCKS ME! I'LL DESTROY IT AND BE FREE OF IT FOREVER!
21
AAAAEEE! OOOOH!
22
WHAT WAS THAT HORRIBLE SOUND? OH, DORI! IS THAT YOU? GET UP!

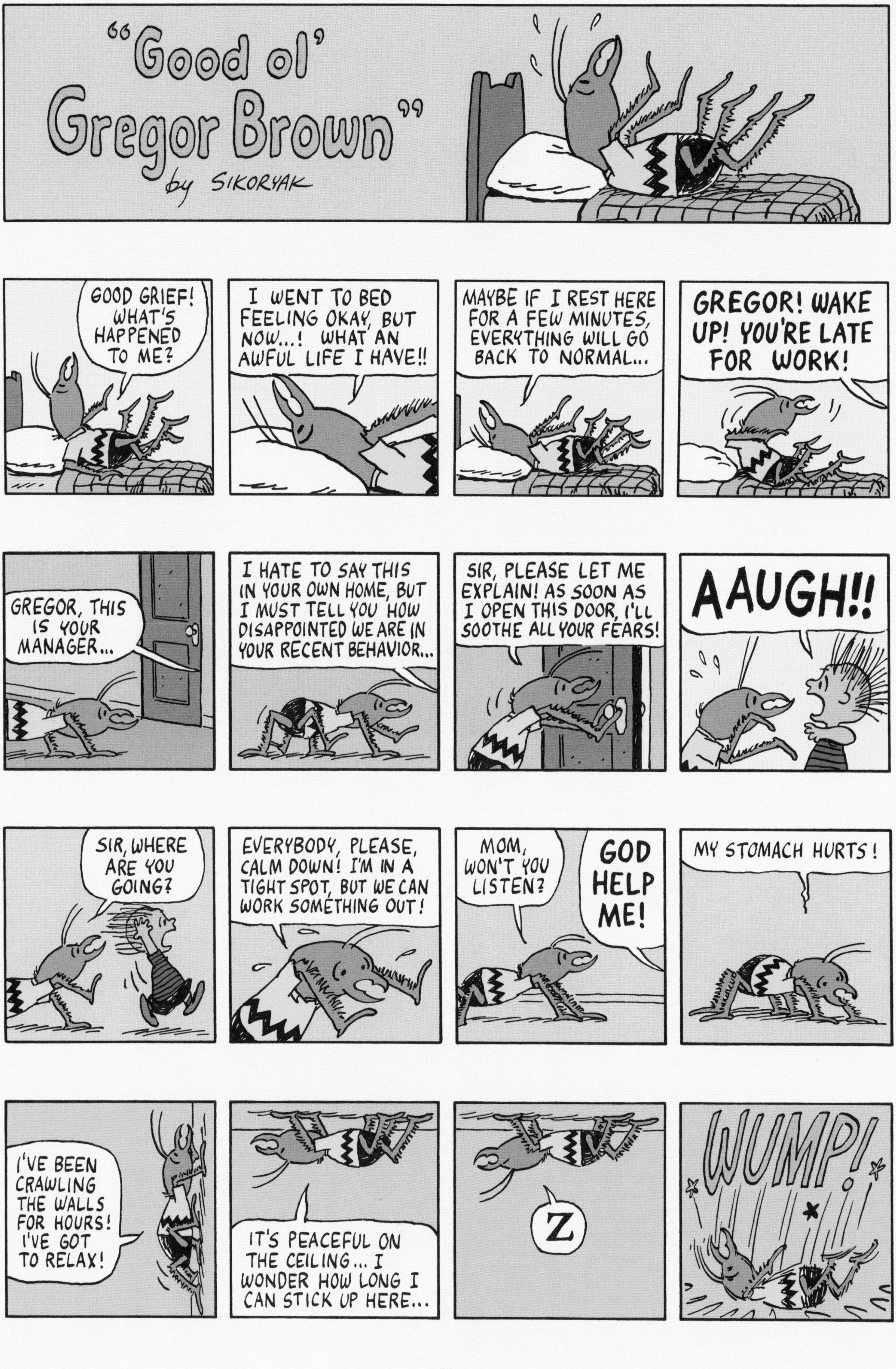
"Good ol' Gregor Brown"
by SIKORYAK
GOOD GRIEF! WHAT'S HAPPENED TO ME?
I WENT TO BED FEELING OKAY, BUT NOW...! WHAT AN AWFUL LIFE I HAVE!!
MAYBE IF I REST HERE FOR A FEW MINUTES, EVERYTHING WILL GO BACK TO NORMAL...
GREGOR! WAKE UP! YOU'RE LATE FOR WORK!
GREGOR, THIS IS YOUR MANAGER...
I HATE TO SAY THIS IN YOUR OWN HOME, BUT I MUST TELL YOU HOW DISAPPOINTED WE ARE IN YOUR RECENT BEHAVIOR...
SIR, PLEASE LET ME EXPLAIN! AS SOON AS I OPEN THIS DOOR, I'LL SOOTHE ALL YOUR FEARS!
AAUGH!!
SIR, WHERE ARE YOU GOING?
EVERYBODY, PLEASE, CALM DOWN! I'M IN A TIGHT SPOT, BUT WE CAN WORK SOMETHING OUT!
MOM, WON'T YOU LISTEN?
GOD HELP ME!
MY STOMACH HURTS!
I'VE BEEN CRAWLING THE WALLS FOR HOURS! I'VE GOT TO RELAX!
IT'S PEACEFUL ON THE CEILING... I WONDER HOW LONG I CAN STICK UP HERE...
Z
WUMP!

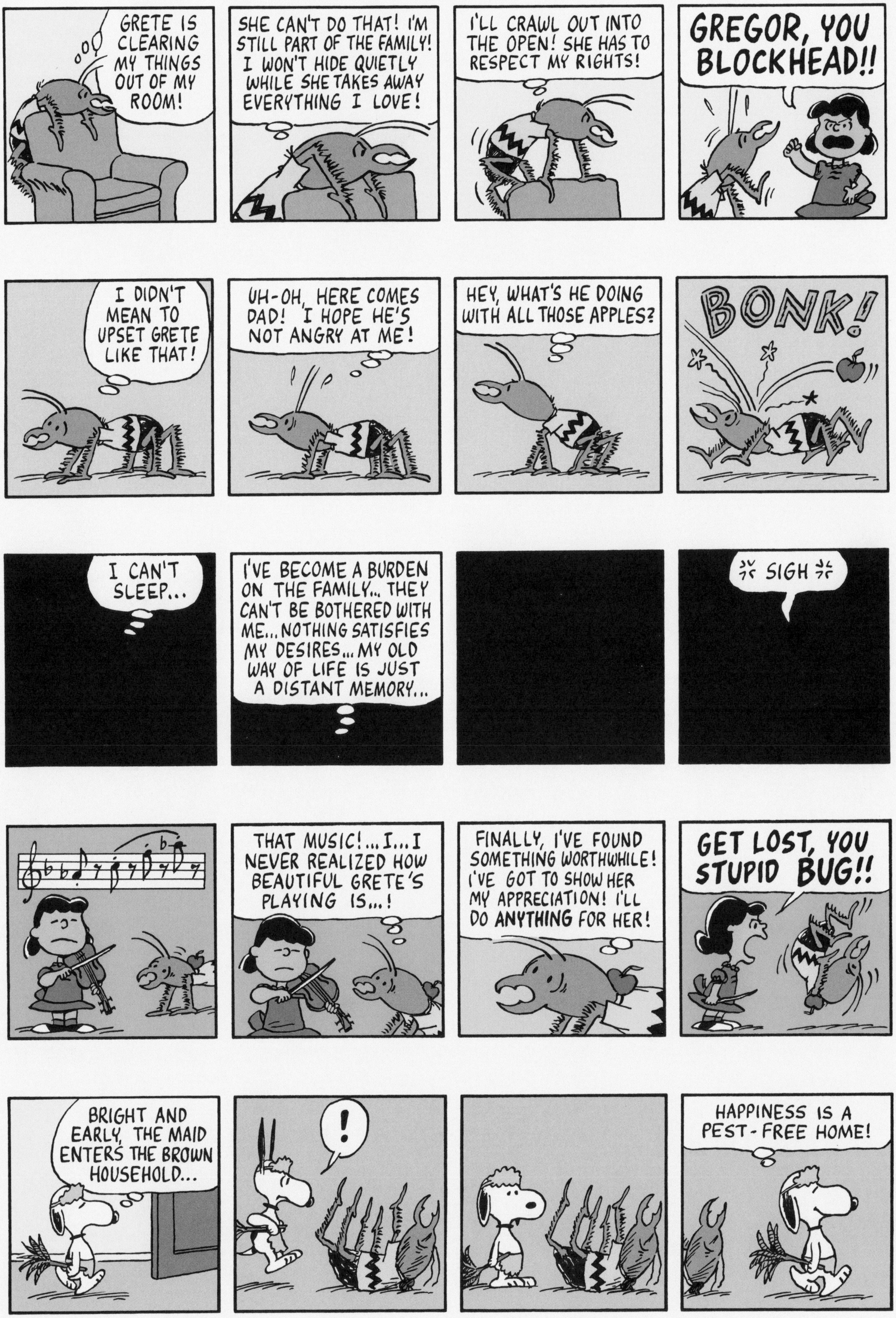
GRETE IS CLEARING MY THINGS OUT OF MY ROOM!
SHE CAN'T DO THAT! I'M STILL PART OF THE FAMILY! I WON'T HIDE QUIETLY WHILE SHE TAKES AWAY EVERYTHING I LOVE!
I'LL CRAWL OUT INTO THE OPEN! SHE HAS TO RESPECT MY RIGHTS!
GREGOR, YOU BLOCKHEAD!!
I DIDN'T MEAN TO UPSET GRETE LIKE THAT!
UH-OH, HERE COMES DAD! I HOPE HE'S NOT ANGRY AT ME!
HEY, WHAT'S HE DOING WITH ALL THOSE APPLES?
BONK!
I CAN'T SLEEP...
I'VE BECOME A BURDEN ON THE FAMILY... THEY CAN'T BE BOTHERED WITH ME... NOTHING SATISFIES MY DESIRES... MY OLD WAY OF LIFE IS JUST A DISTANT MEMORY...
SIGH
THAT MUSIC! ... I... I NEVER REALIZED HOW BEAUTIFUL GRETE'S PLAYING IS...!
FINALLY, I'VE FOUND SOMETHING WORTHWHILE! I'VE GOT TO SHOW HER MY APPRECIATION! I'LL DO ANYTHING FOR HER!
GET LOST, YOU STUPID BUG!!
BRIGHT AND EARLY, THE MAID ENTERS THE BROWN HOUSEHOLD...
!
HAPPINESS IS A PEST-FREE HOME!

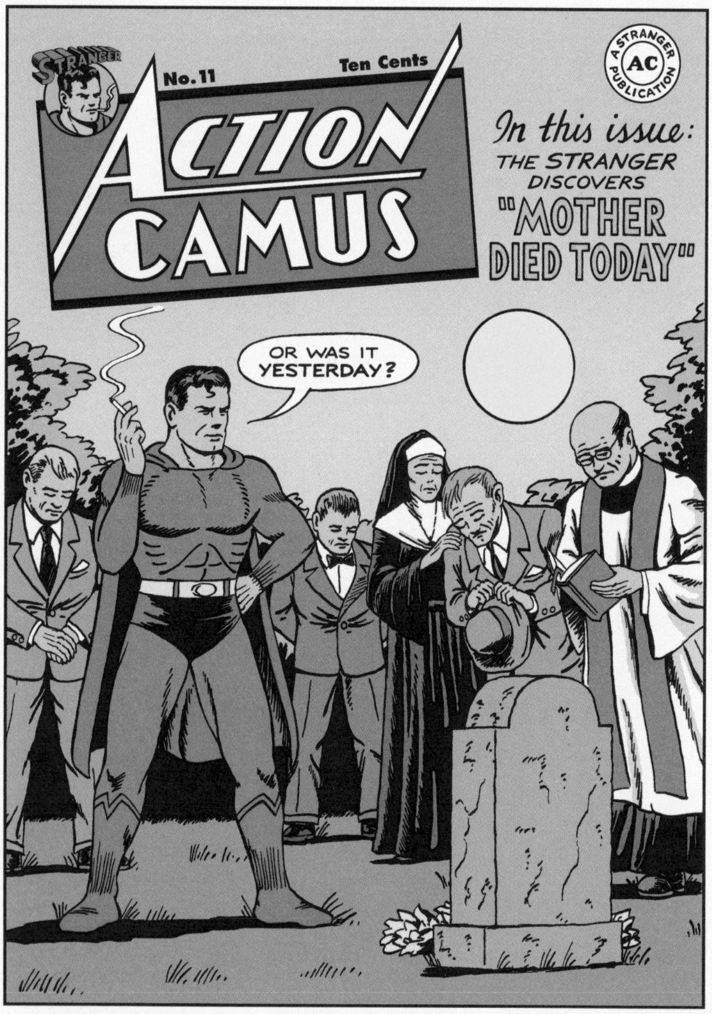
STRANGER
No. 11
Ten Cents
A STRANGER PUBLICATION AC
ACTION CAMUS
In this issue: THE STRANGER DISCOVERS "MOTHER DIED TODAY"
OR WAS IT YESTERDAY?

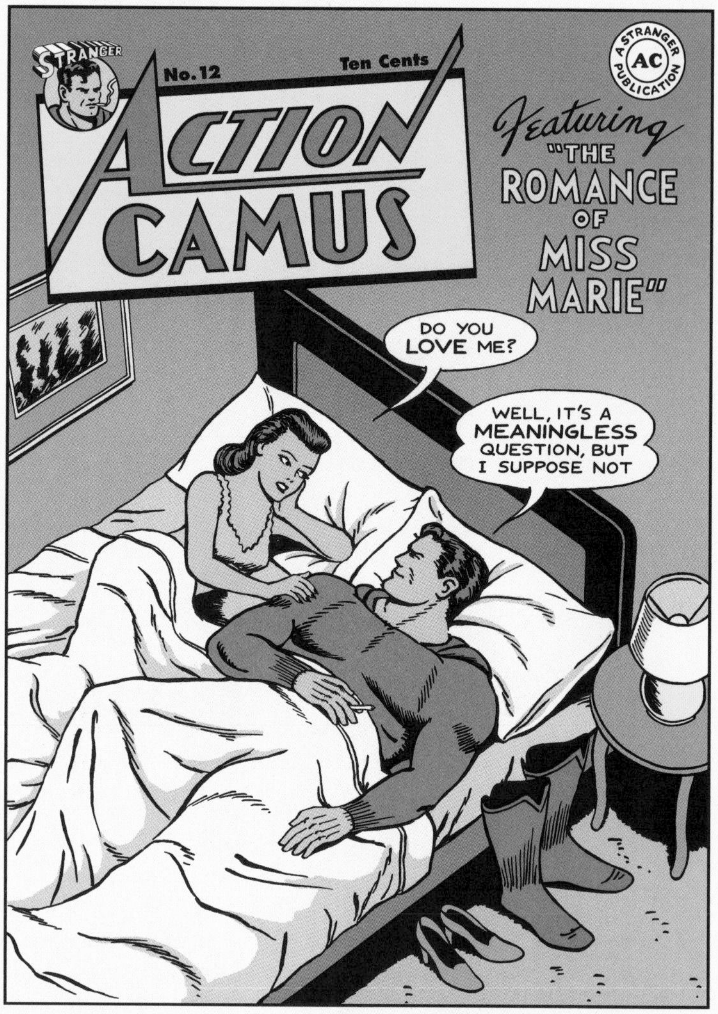
STRANGER
No. 12
Ten Cents
A STRANGER PUBLICATION AC
ACTION CAMUS
Featuring "THE ROMANCE OF MISS MARIE"
DO YOU LOVE ME?
WELL, IT'S A MEANINGLESS QUESTION, BUT I SUPPOSE NOT

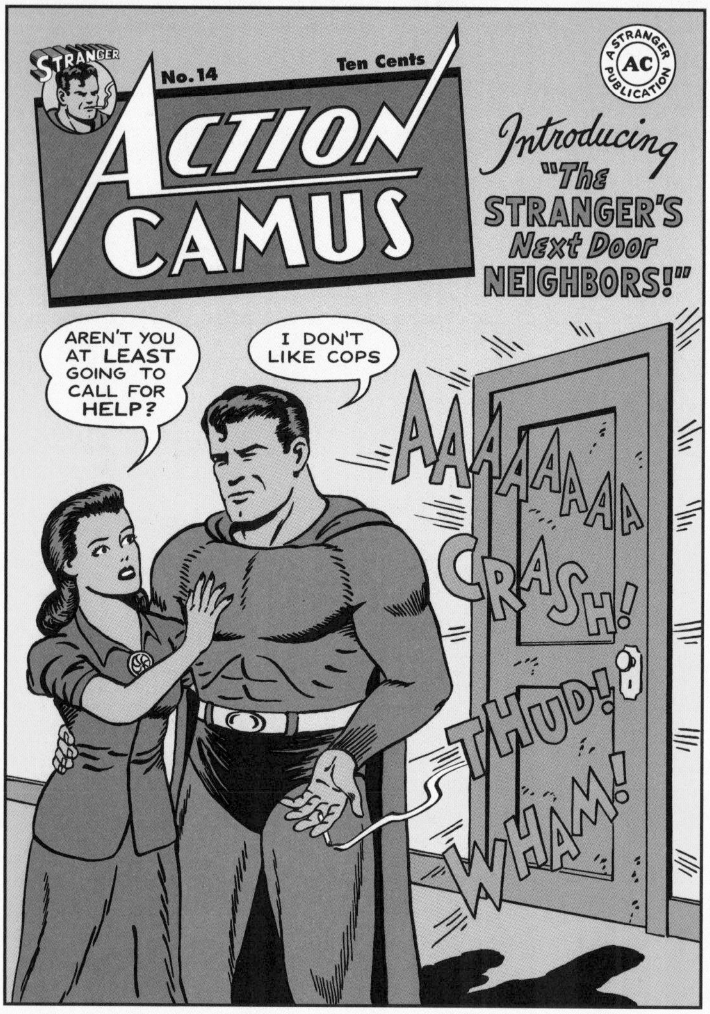
STRANGER
No. 14
Ten Cents
A STRANGER PUBLICATION AC
ACTION CAMUS
Introducing "The STRANGER'S Next Door NEIGHBORS!"
AREN'T YOU AT LEAST GOING TO CALL FOR HELP?
I DON'T LIKE COPS
AAAAAAAA
CRASH!
THUD!
WHAM!

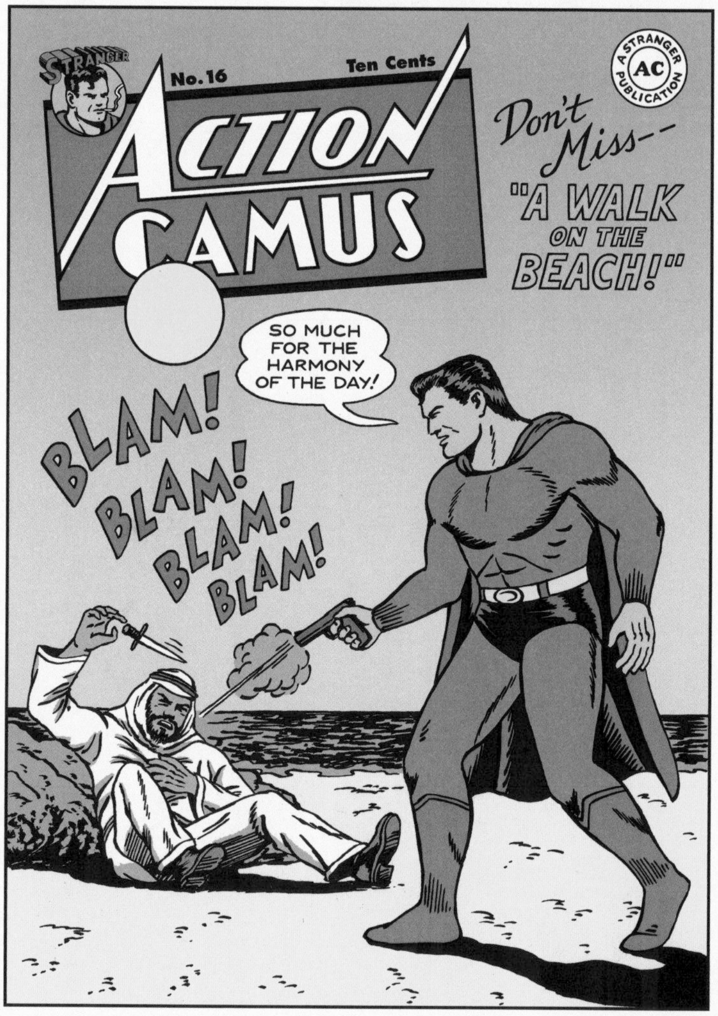
STRANGER
No. 16
Ten Cents
A STRANGER PUBLICATION AC
ACTION CAMUS
Don't Miss-- "A WALK ON THE BEACH!"
SO MUCH FOR THE HARMONY OF THE DAY!
BLAM!
BLAM!
BLAM!
BLAM!

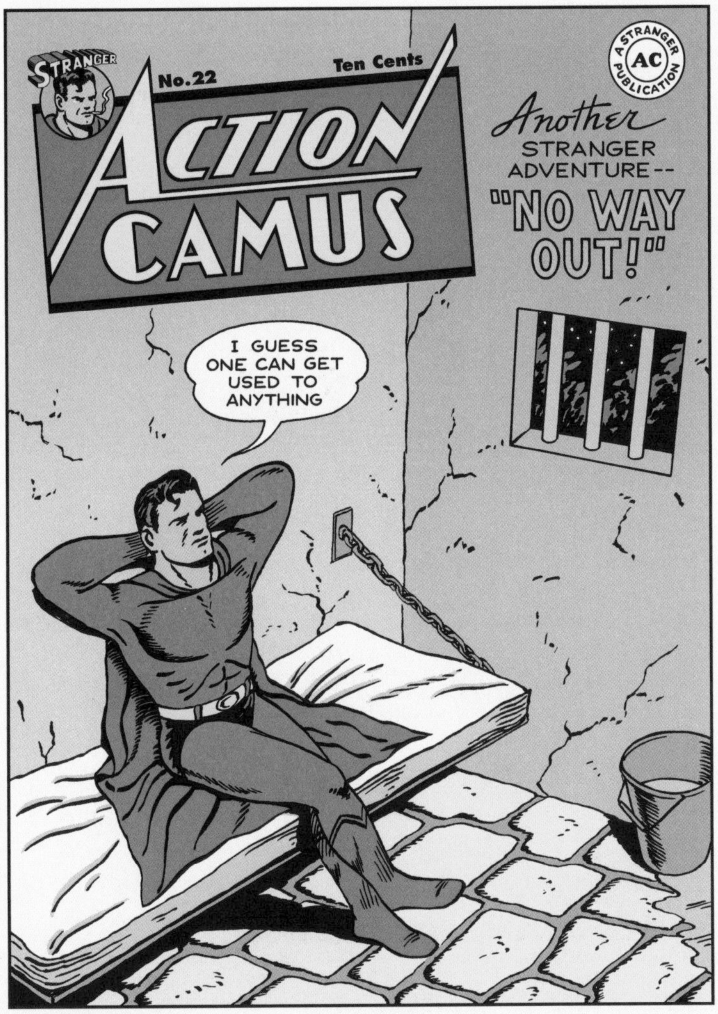
STRANGER
No.22
Ten Cents
A STRANGER PUBLICATION
AC
ACTION CAMUS
Another STRANGER ADVENTURE-- "NO WAY OUT!"
I GUESS ONE CAN GET USED TO ANYTHING

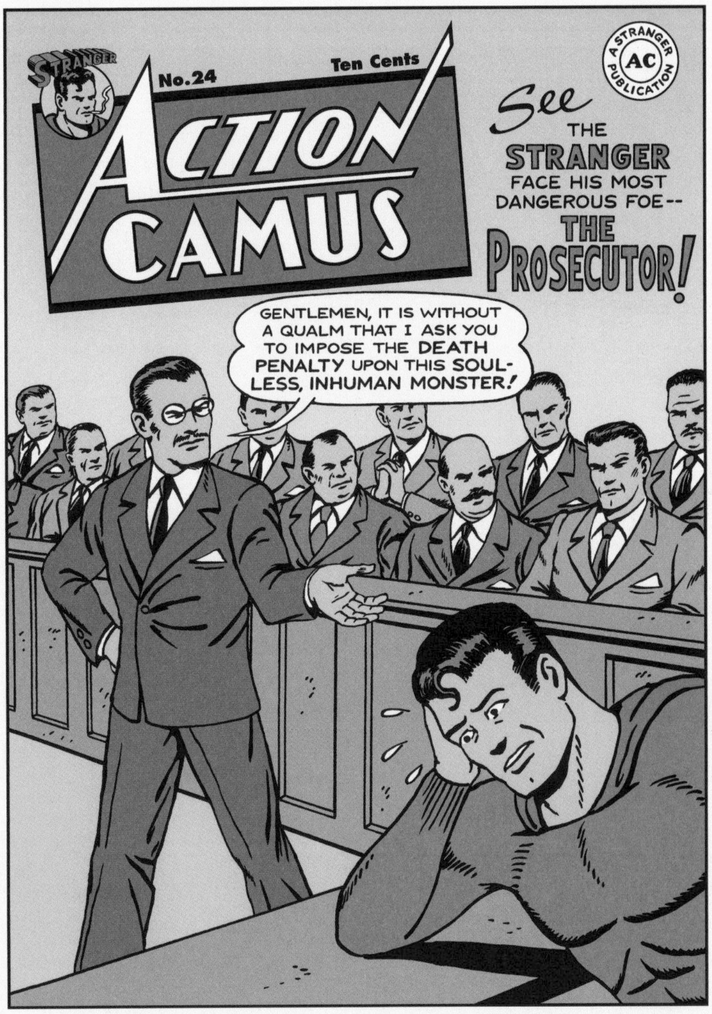
STRANGER
No.24
Ten Cents
A STRANGER PUBLICATION
AC
ACTION CAMUS
See THE STRANGER FACE HIS MOST DANGEROUS FOE-- THE PROSECUTOR!
GENTLEMEN, IT IS WITHOUT A QUALM THAT I ASK YOU TO IMPOSE THE DEATH PENALTY UPON THIS SOUL-LESS, INHUMAN MONSTER!

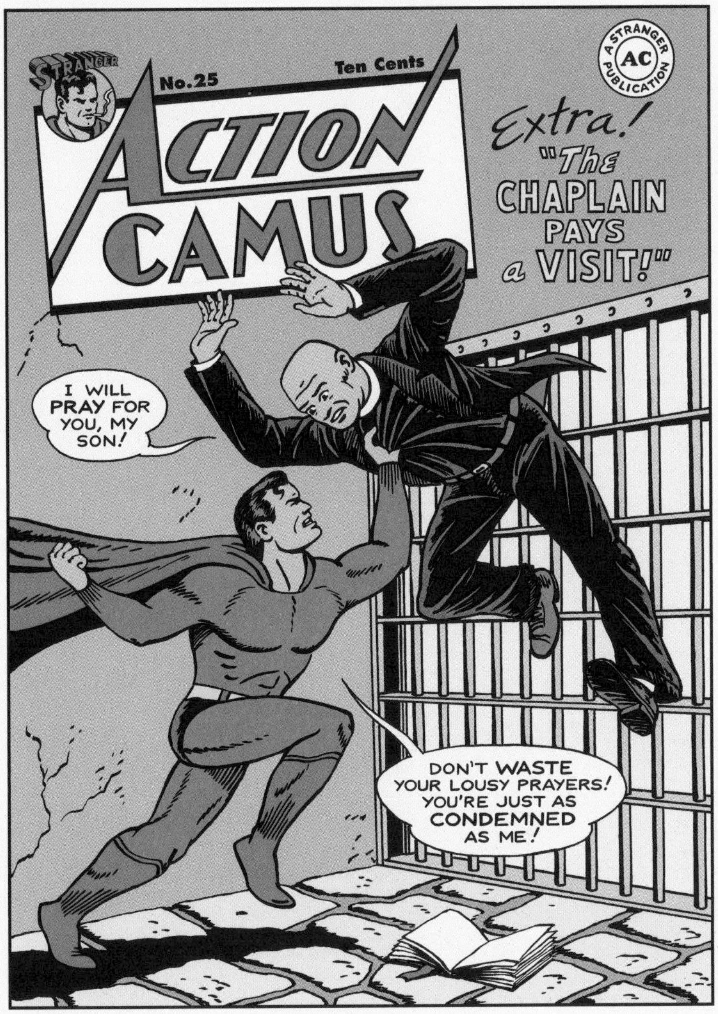
STRANGER
No.25
Ten Cents
A STRANGER PUBLICATION
AC
ACTION CAMUS
Extra! "The CHAPLAIN PAYS a VISIT!"
I WILL PRAY FOR YOU, MY SON!
DON'T WASTE YOUR LOUSY PRAYERS! YOU'RE JUST AS CONDEMNED AS ME!

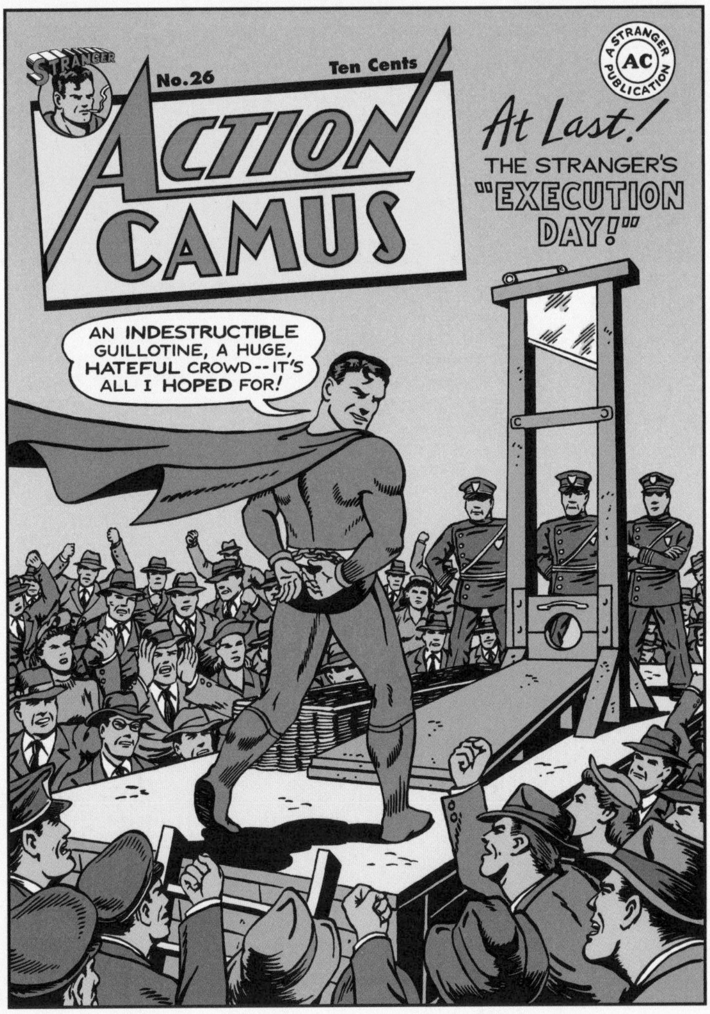
STRANGER
No.26
Ten Cents
A STRANGER PUBLICATION
AC
ACTION CAMUS
At Last! THE STRANGER'S "EXECUTION DAY!"
AN INDESTRUCTIBLE GUILLOTINE, A HUGE, HATEFUL CROWD--IT'S ALL I HOPED FOR!

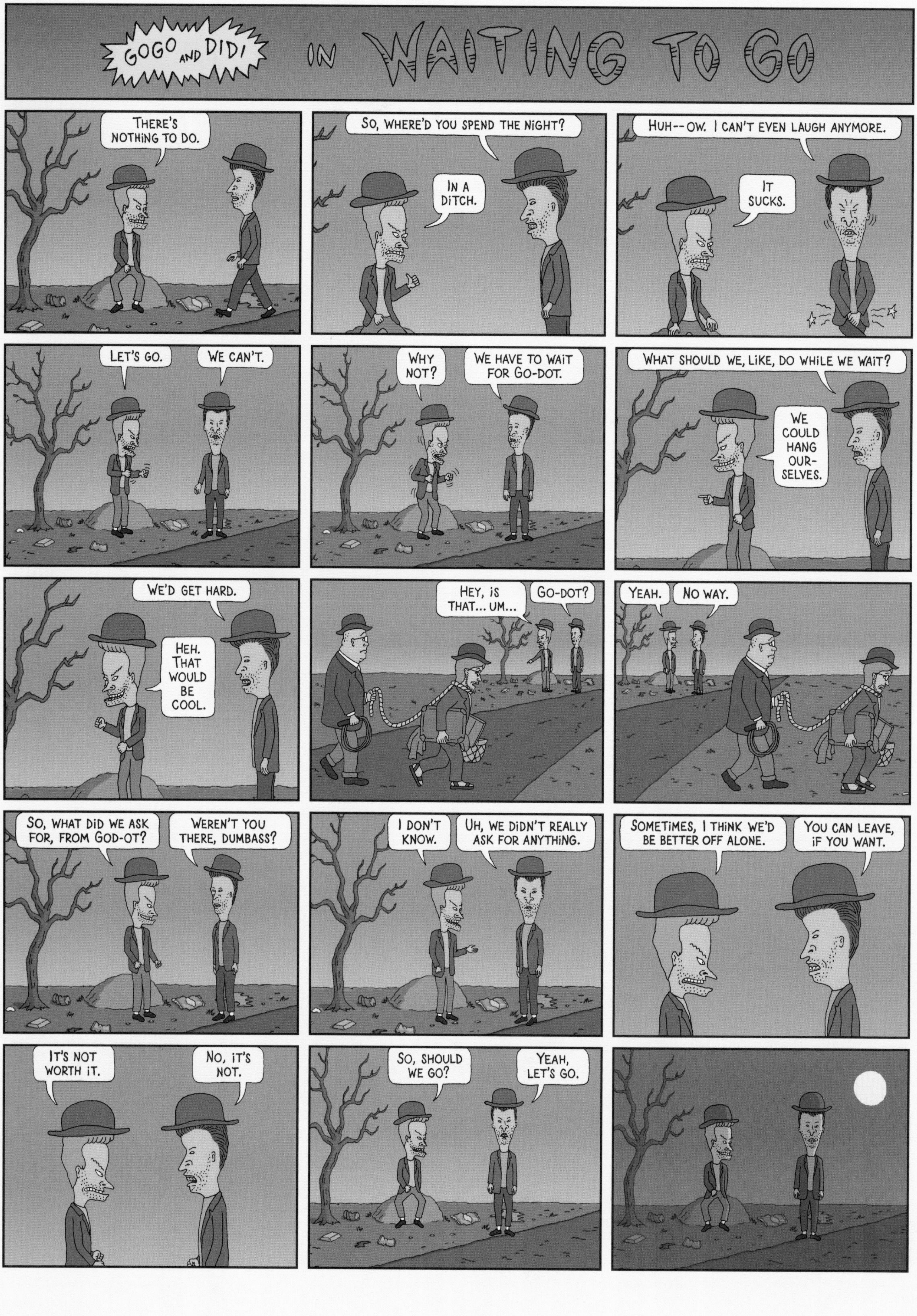
GOGO AND DIDI
IN WAITING TO GO
THERE'S NOTHING TO DO.
SO, WHERE'D YOU SPEND THE NIGHT?
IN A DITCH.
HUH--OW. I CAN'T EVEN LAUGH ANYMORE.
IT SUCKS.
LET'S GO.
WE CAN'T.
WHY NOT?
WE HAVE TO WAIT FOR GO-DOT.
WHAT SHOULD WE, LIKE, DO WHILE WE WAIT?
WE COULD HANG OUR-SELVES.
WE'D GET HARD.
HEH. THAT WOULD BE COOL.
HEY, IS THAT... UM...
GO-DOT?
YEAH.
NO WAY.
SO, WHAT DID WE ASK FOR, FROM GOD-OT?
WEREN'T YOU THERE, DUMBASS?
I DON'T KNOW.
UH, WE DIDN'T REALLY ASK FOR ANYTHING.
SOMETIMES, I THINK WE'D BE BETTER OFF ALONE.
YOU CAN LEAVE, IF YOU WANT.
IT'S NOT WORTH IT.
NO, IT'S NOT.
SO, SHOULD WE GO?
YEAH, LET'S GO.

Masterpiece QUERIES

Have a question about a story? Send your letters to: Professor Scholar c/o the publisher.

Dear Prof. S.,

I've been puzzled by one fellow in LITTLE PEARL – isn't Chilly a little small to be married to Hester? — E. A. Duyck, NY, NY

Well, remember that he is in disguise. His stature was suggested by a round little fellow who appeared in a long running series of humorous "comic books" by John Stanley and Irving Tripp, based on characters created by Marjorie Henderson Buell in 1935. Those picto-narratives starred a kind but mischievous young girl, her neighborhood friends, and her family. There are several parallels between Nathaniel Hawthorne's 1850 dark romantic novel and Stanley and Tripp's stories, in which the children are forever competing among themselves and scheming against the adults. In particular, the aforementioned round little fellow is continually accusing the heroine's father of one crime or another.

To the Professor,

In DOSTOYEVSKY COMICS, why does Raskol turn himself in? He's very clever. Couldn't he just escape from the cops? — Nik Strakhov, Saint Petersburg, RU

Perhaps you were thinking of the nocturnal hero created by Bob Kane and Bill Finger in 1939. That winged-mammal-character is actually a rich American playboy who takes the law into his own hands to create a better world. In contrast, the protagonist of Fyodor Dostoyevsky's 1866 serialized novel is a poor Russian student who takes the law into his own hands to create a better world. The parallels, even down to their respective supporting casts, are numerous and fascinating. For instance, Kane and Finger's hero, as a young boy, witnessed the murder of his parents, which inspired his battle for justice. Dostoyevsky's hero dreams that, as a child, he saw the beating of a horse, which precedes his own violent actions. Still, only one of these characters has consistently avoided capture, and he's the one who has inspired a series of hit movies and television shows, as well as an incredibly successful line of action figures and fast food tie-ins.

Dear Prof. S.,

The painting's transformation in LITTLE DORI is startling. Was it caused by Dori's wish in panel two? — Joe M.S., Philadelphia, PA

Precisely. In Oscar Wilde's 1891 Gothic horror novel, as in Winsor McCay's colorful Sunday comics of 1905-1927, the hero's

dreams become vivid and real. The only crucial difference between the characters is that Wilde's boy wants to debase himself while McCay's boy wants to meet a princess. In both of these narratives, the natural world reasserts itself after many adventures, but only McCay's boy has to face reality, get out of bed, and take a bath.

Dear P.S.,

I feel terrible for the poor guy in GREGOR BROWN. Wasn't there anything he could do to save himself? — Max B., Prague, CZ

Not likely. As with the bald-headed protagonist of Charles M. Schulz' long running comic strip (1950-2000), the famous character from Franz Kafka's 1915 short story has very bad luck. Despite their sincere efforts, circumstances always seem to conspire against them — whether they're playing a baseball game with a quarrelsome team, or waking up as a dung beetle with a quarrelsome family.

Hello Professor Scholar,

Would you explain why the sun is so large on two of the ACTION CAMUS covers? — Gaston G., Paris, FR

In Albert Camus' 1942 absurdist-existential novel, the sun is a great source of power which deeply affects his protagonist, even spurring him to action. In this way, it recalls the sun's influence on the powerful comic book protagonist created by Jerry Siegel and Joe Shuster, who first appeared in 1938. Supposedly this muscular being from another world derived his considerable strength from our yellow sun. In contrast with Camus' hero, he seemed a little more comfortable in Western society.

Dear Professor,

Those two guys in WAITING TO GO remind me of The Katzenjammer Kids. — R. Blin, Paris, FR

I suppose so, but we were thinking of the Mike Judge's 1992 duo, the stars of television, film, and books. Their world and complex relationship precisely echo those in Samuel Beckett's 1952 modernist play. Still, you bring up an interesting point; these two may resonate to some degree with Hans & Fritz Katzenjammer, as well as Mutt & Jeff, Fred & Barney, Archie & Jughead, the Thing & the Hulk... but perhaps that's a discussion for another time.

Coming soon: Virgil! Chaucer! Flaubert! And more! Watch for them at your newsstand or local library!

R. Sikoryak has drawn cartoons for numerous media giants, including *Nickelodeon Magazine*, *The New Yorker*, and *The Daily Show with Jon Stewart*, as well as for independent publications, films, and theater productions. His cartoon slide show series *Carousel* has been presented around the U.S. and Canada. He also teaches and lectures on comics and illustration. Sikoryak lives in New York City with his wife and frequent collaborator Kriota Willberg.